The Ultimate
Air Fryer Cookbook UK

Budget-Friendly and Yummy Air Fryer Meals for Beginners
With Easy to Follow Instructions to Maximise the Use of Your
Air Fryer(2023 Edition)

Carol M. McKinney

Contents

Introduction

Air fryers have taken the culinary world by storm, and for good reason. As a cooking enthusiast, I was initially skeptical about the hype surrounding air fryers, but once I tried one for myself, I was pleasantly surprised.

Health-conscious cooks will appreciate that air fryers offer a healthier alternative to deep frying. By using just a small amount of oil, or even none at all, you can enjoy all your favorite fried foods without sacrificing flavor or texture. Plus, the cleanup is a breeze compared to traditional frying methods.

But beyond the convenience and health benefits, air fryers also open up a world of culinary possibilities. They allow you to experiment with new flavors, textures, and cooking techniques, from the perfect sear on a steak to the crispiest potato chips you've ever tasted.

My goal as the author of this guide is to equip you with the necessary tools and knowledge to fully utilize your air fryer. Rest assured, this book is a product of my fervent love for cooking and admiration for the air fryer. Within its pages, I have included my personal collection of recipes and insightful tips that I have gathered over time, so that others can reap the same benefits that I have.

So whether you're a seasoned chef or a beginner in the kitchen, I hope this guide will inspire you to discover the magic of air fryers and enjoy healthier, tastier cooking.

What is Air Fryers?

Air fryers are a type of kitchen appliance that uses hot air to cook food, creating a crispy and fried-like texture without the need for excessive oil. They are a relatively new addition to the market and have gained immense popularity due to their convenience and health benefits.

The mechanism of air fryers involves circulating hot air around the food placed in a basket or tray. This hot air cooks the food from all angles, resulting in a crispy texture similar to that achieved by deep frying. The air fryer uses a heating element to heat the air and a fan to circulate it around the food. This mechanism allows for even cooking and eliminates the need for flipping or stirring the food during the cooking process.

Why You Should Consider Owning One?

Are you tired of spending hours in the kitchen preparing meals that aren't as healthy or delicious as you'd like? Have you been searching for a cooking appliance that can help you save time and make your favorite foods with less mess? If so, it's time to consider owning an air fryer.Here are 8 reasons why you should consider owning an air fryer:

·**Healthy Cuisine**

Air fryers use hot air to cook food, meaning they require little to no oil to produce crispy, golden results. This makes them an excellent alternative to traditional deep frying methods, as they significantly reduce the amount of fat and calories in your food.

·**Time Efficiency**

Air fryers are an incredibly efficient way to cook food quickly. They preheat in just a few minutes, and most foods cook in less than 20 minutes. This makes them perfect for those who are short on time but still want to enjoy a home-cooked meal.

·**User-Friendly**

Air fryers are incredibly user-friendly. Simply set the temperature and cooking time, and the appliance will do the rest. They require minimal monitoring, and most models have a built-in timer and automatic shut-off feature.

·Versatile

Air fryers can be used to cook a wide range of foods, including chicken, fish, vegetables, and even desserts. They can also be used to reheat leftovers, defrost frozen foods, and bake.

·Less Mess

Unlike traditional deep frying, air fryers don't require a large amount of oil, meaning there is less mess to clean up. Additionally, most air fryer baskets and trays are dishwasher safe, making clean-up a breeze.

·Energy Efficient

Air fryers use significantly less energy than traditional ovens and deep fryers, making them an eco-friendly option. They also don't heat up the entire kitchen, making them a great option for hot summer days.

·Fry Yummylicious Frozen Finger Foods

Air fryers are perfect for making frozen finger foods crispy and delicious without deep frying in oil. This is a healthier option as it reduces the amount of oil and calories absorbed during cooking. Air frying frozen finger foods is also much faster and easier than using a conventional oven, making it a great option for busy individuals who want to enjoy tasty and nutritious snacks.

·Affordable

While some air fryer models can be expensive, there are plenty of affordable options on the market. Investing in an air fryer can also save you money in the long run, as you won't need to purchase as much cooking oil or other cooking supplies.

What Delicious Things Can You Cook?

Air fryers excel in one area above all else: creating irresistibly crispy and delectable dishes that are rich in flavor and packed with nutrients.However, for those who are new to air frying, it can be challenging to know where to start. Fortunately, the possibilities are endless, and air fryers can be used to create a wide range of meals.

One common question beginners often have is, "What can I cook in my air fryer?" The answer is that there are countless options. From crispy chicken wings and juicy steaks to flaky fish and golden-brown onion rings, air fryers are versatile and can handle a variety of dishes. With a little experimentation, you can discover your favorite air fryer recipes and enjoy healthy and delicious meals.Here are 8 delicious and nutritious foods to cook in an air fryer:

Chicken: Air fried chicken is juicy on the inside and crispy on the outside, with less oil than traditional fried chicken.

Fish: Air frying fish creates a perfectly crispy exterior and a moist, flaky interior, without any greasy residue.

Vegetables: Air frying vegetables such as Brussels sprouts, cauliflower, and broccoli is a great way to make them crispy and caramelized while retaining their nutritional value.

French fries: Air fried French fries are crispy on the outside and soft on the inside, with less oil and fewer calories than deep-fried versions.

Bacon: Air frying bacon results in perfectly crispy bacon without the mess of grease splatters.

Donuts: Air frying donuts creates a crispy exterior and a soft, fluffy interior without the need for deep frying.

Tofu: Air frying tofu creates a crispy exterior and a tender interior, making it a great plant-based protein option.

Baked goods: Air fryers can also be used to bake a variety of desserts such as muffins, cakes, and brownies with less fat and fewer calories than traditional baking methods. These are just a few examples of the many delicious and healthy foods you can cook in an air fryer. With a little creativity, you can air fry almost anything and enjoy the same delicious results with fewer calories and less fat Foods to Skipin an Air Fryer In this article, we'll explore six types of foods that you should skip in an air fryer to avoid disappointment, damage, or health risks.

Wet Batter Coated Foods

While it's tempting to try to replicate your favorite deep-fried foods in an air fryer, wet batter-coated foods like fish and chips or chicken nuggets don't turn out as well as you'd hope. The batter tends to drip off the food and accumulate in the bottom of the air fryer, causing smoke and mess. Moreover, the batter doesn't crisp up as it would in hot oil, resulting in a soggy and unappetizing texture.

Raw Vegetables

While some vegetables can be cooked in the air fryer, raw vegetables such as broccoli or cauliflower may not turn out well. The hot air may not cook them evenly, resulting in some parts being overcooked while others are undercooked.

Cheese

While it may be tempting to try and make cheese sticks or cheese-filled snacks in the air fryer, the result is often a messy and gooey mess. Cheese can melt and drip in the air fryer, making it difficult to clean and creating a fire hazard.

Delicate Seafood

Foods that are delicate or easily breakable, such as soft tofu or flaky fish, may not hold up well in the air fryer. The strong hot air circulating in the air fryer can cause delicate foods to break apart or become overcooked.

High-Fat Meats

Air fryers are great for cooking lean meats such as chicken breasts or fish, but high-fat meats such as bacon or sausage tend to splatter and create a mess in the air fryer. Additionally, the excess fat can cause smoke and unpleasant odors.

Anything with a Liquid Marinade

Marinating is an excellent way to add flavor and tenderness to meats or vegetables before cooking. However, when it comes to air frying, anything with a liquid marinade should be avoided. Liquid marinades tend to drip off the food and accumulate in the bottom of the air fryer, causing smoke and mess. Moreover, the liquid can interfere with the hot air circulation and cause the food to cook unevenly or become soggy.

Potential Safety Concerns

There are some potential risks associated with using them. It's important to be aware of these risks so that you can take appropriate precautions when using your air fryer.

One of the main risks associated with air fryers is the potential for burns. Air fryers use very hot air to cook food, and if you're not careful, you could accidentally burn yourself. To reduce the risk of burns, always use oven mitts or heat-resistant gloves when handling your air fryer or its accessories.

Another risk associated with air fryers is the potential for fires. Air fryers can generate a lot of heat, and if you're not careful, this heat can ignite nearby objects or even start a kitchen fire. To reduce the risk of fires, always use your air fryer on a heat-resistant surface, and never leave it unattended while it's in use.

Additionally, some studies suggest that cooking with air fryers could produce harmful chemicals such as acrylamide, which is a known carcinogen. While the risks associated with these chemicals are still being studied, it's important to be aware of their potential presence and take steps to minimize your exposure. One way to do this is by cooking with lower temperatures and shorter cooking times. Finally, some people may be sensitive to the fumes produced by air fryers, particularly if they have respiratory issues such as asthma. To reduce the risk of respiratory problems, make sure to use your air fryer in a well-ventilated area.

To fully enjoy the many benefits of cooking with an air fryer, it's important to be aware of the potential risks that come with it. While air fryers are generally safe and easy to use, taking appropriate precautions and following the manufacturer's instructions can help minimize your risk of injury or illness.

Maintaining and Cleaning Your Air Fryer

In this guide, we will go over the step-by-step process of cleaning and maintaining your air fryer.

Step 1: Unplug the Air Fryer

Before cleaning your air fryer, always unplug it from the power source to ensure your safety.

Step 2: Remove any Excess Food or Debris

After the air fryer has cooled down, remove any excess food or debris from the basket or tray. Use a soft-bristled brush or sponge to remove any food particles that are stuck to the basket or tray. Be careful not to scratch the surface of the basket or tray.

Step 3: Soak the Basket and Tray

Next, fill a sink with warm soapy water and soak the basket and tray for at least 10-15 minutes. This will help to loosen any remaining food particles.

Step 4: Clean the Basket and Tray

After soaking, use a non-abrasive sponge or cloth to clean the basket and tray thoroughly. Pay attention to the corners and crevices where food particles tend to accumulate.

Step 5: Rinse and Dry the Basket and Tray

Once the basket and tray are clean, rinse them with clean water and dry them with a clean cloth or paper towel. Ensure that there is no water left on the surface of the basket and tray.

Step 6: Clean the Exterior

Use a soft cloth or sponge to clean the exterior of the air fryer. Do not use harsh chemicals or abrasive sponges as this may damage the surface of the air fryer.

Step 7: Clean the Heating Element

The heating element is the component that heats up the air inside the air fryer. To clean the heating element, use a soft-bristled brush or a toothbrush to remove any debris or food particles that may have accumulated.

Step 8: Reassemble the Air Fryer

After cleaning, reassemble the air fryer according to the manufacturer's instructions. Ensure that all the parts are properly aligned and securely in place.

Step 9: Store the Air Fryer

Once the air fryer is completely dry, store it in a clean, dry place. Avoid storing the air fryer in a damp or humid place.

Regular maintenance and cleaning of your air fryer will ensure that it remains in good working condition for years to come. By following these simple steps, you can keep your air fryer in good working condition for years to come.

Air Fryers Safety Tricks and Tips

While air fryers are generally safe to use, it's important to take precautions to ensure that you use them correctly and avoid accidents.

Here are some safety tricks and tips to keep in mind when using an air fryer:

·**Read the manual**

Before using your air fryer, read the manual carefully to understand how to use it safely and correctly.

·**Don't overload the basket**

Overloading the basket can lead to uneven cooking and potentially dangerous hot spots. Stick to the recommended capacity and spread food out in a single layer for even cooking.

·**Use oven mitts:**

The basket and accessories of an air fryer can get hot during cooking, so always use oven mitts or heat-resistant gloves when handling them.

·**Keep it on a flat, stable surface**

Place your air fryer on a flat, stable surface to prevent it from tipping over during use.

·**Don't put anything on top of the air fryer**

Keep the top of the air fryer clear to allow for proper ventilation and prevent overheating.

·**Keep it away from water**

Never use an air fryer near water or submerge it in water, as it can cause electric shock.

·**Check the cord**

Regularly check the cord and plug for any signs of damage, such as fraying or exposed wires. If you notice any damage, stop using the air fryer and contact the manufacturer for a replacement.

·**Clean it regularly**

Proper cleaning is important for maintaining the performance and safety of your air fryer. Refer to the manual for specific cleaning instructions, but in general, wipe down the basket and accessories with a damp cloth after each use, and deep clean the interior and exterior of the air fryer on a regular basis.

By following these safety tricks and tips, you can enjoy cooking with your air fryer while minimizing the risk of accidents and ensuring that it continues to perform at its best.

Air Fryer FAQ

1. Can I cook multiple foods at the same time in an air fryer?

Yes, you can cook multiple foods at the same time in an air fryer, as long as they require the same cooking temperature and time. Just be sure to arrange the food in a single layer and leave some space between each item for the hot air to circulate.

2. How do I prevent my food from sticking to the air fryer basket?

To prevent food from sticking to the air fryer basket, make sure to lightly coat the food with oil before placing it in the basket. You can also try using a non-stick spray or lining the basket with parchment paper.

3.Can I use aluminum foil in my air fryer?

Yes, you can use aluminum foil in your air fryer, but make sure to use it sparingly and avoid covering the entire basket, as this can block airflow and affect the cooking process.

4.How often should I clean my air fryer?

It's recommended to clean your air fryer after each use. This will prevent buildup of grease and food particles and ensure that your air fryer lasts longer.

5.Can I use my air fryer to bake?

Yes, you can use your air fryer to bake. Just make sure to use an appropriate baking pan that fits inside the air fryer basket, and adjust the cooking time and temperature accordingly.

6.How do I avoid overcooking my food in the air fryer?

To avoid overcooking your food in the air fryer, make sure to check it periodically during the cooking process and adjust the time and temperature as needed. You can also use a food thermometer to check for doneness.

7.How long do I need to cook food in an air fryer?

Cooking times can vary depending on the type of food and the size of the portion. Always refer to the manufacturer's instructions or a recipe for guidance on cooking times and temperatures. It's also a good idea to check the food frequently while cooking to avoid overcooking or burning.

CHAPTER 1 BREAKFAST RECIPES

Cheddar Soufflés

Serves 4

Prep time: 15 minutes / Cook time: 12 minutes

Ingredients:

- 3 large eggs, whites and yolks separated
- ¼ teaspoon cream of tartar
- 120 ml shredded sharp Cheddar cheese
- 85 g cream cheese, softened

Instructions:

1. In a large bowl, beat egg whites together with cream of tartar until soft peaks form, about 2 minutes.
2. In a separate medium bowl, beat egg yolks, Cheddar, and cream cheese together until frothy, about 1 minute. Add egg yolk mixture to whites, gently folding until combined.
3. Pour mixture evenly into four ramekins greased with cooking spray. Place ramekins into air fryer basket. Adjust the temperature to 176ºC and bake for 12 minutes. Eggs will be browned on the top and firm in the center when done. Serve warm.

Sausage Egg Cup

Serves 6

Prep time: 10 minutes / Cook time: 15 minutes

Ingredients:

- 340 g pork sausage, removed from casings
- 6 large eggs
- ½ teaspoon salt
- ¼ teaspoon ground black pepper
- ½ teaspoon crushed red pepper flakes

Instructions:

1. Place sausage in six 4-inch ramekins (about 60 g per ramekin) greased with cooking oil. Press sausage down to cover bottom and about ½-inch up the sides of ramekins. Crack one egg into each ramekin and sprinkle evenly with salt, black pepper, and red pepper flakes.
2. Place ramekins into air fryer basket. Adjust the temperature to 176ºC and set the timer for 15 minutes. Egg cups will be done when sausage is fully cooked to at least 64ºC and the egg is firm. Serve warm.

Cauliflower Avocado Toast

Serves 2

Prep time: 15 minutes / Cook time: 8 minutes

Ingredients:

- 1 (40 g) steamer bag cauliflower
- 1 large egg
- 120 ml shredded Mozzarella cheese
- 1 ripe medium avocado
- ½ teaspoon garlic powder
- ¼ teaspoon ground black pepper

Instructions:

1. Cook cauliflower according to package instructions. Remove from bag and place into cheesecloth or clean towel to remove excess moisture.
2. Place cauliflower into a large bowl and mix in egg and Mozzarella. Cut a piece of parchment to fit your air fryer basket. Separate the cauliflower mixture into two, and place it on the parchment in two mounds. Press out the cauliflower mounds into a ¼-inch-thick rectangle. Place the parchment into the air fryer basket.
3. Adjust the temperature to 204ºC and set the timer for 8 minutes.

4. Flip the cauliflower halfway through the cooking time.
5. When the timer beeps, remove the parchment and allow the cauliflower to cool 5 minutes.
6. Cut open the avocado and remove the pit. Scoop out the inside, place it in a medium bowl, and mash it with garlic powder and pepper. Spread onto the cauliflower. Serve immediately.

Gold Avocado

Serves 4

Prep time: 5 minutes / Cook time: 6 minutes

Ingredients:

- 2 large avocados, sliced
- ¼ teaspoon paprika
- Salt and ground black pepper, to taste
- 120 ml flour
- 2 eggs, beaten
- 235 ml bread crumbs

Instructions:

1. Preheat the air fryer to 204°C.
2. Sprinkle paprika, salt and pepper on the slices of avocado.
3. Lightly coat the avocados with flour. Dredge them in the eggs, before covering with bread crumbs.
4. Transfer to the air fryer and air fry for 6 minutes.
5. Serve warm.

Vanilla Granola

Serves 4

Prep time: 5 minutes / Cook time: 40 minutes

Ingredients:

- 235 ml rolled oats
- 3 tablespoons maple syrup
- 1 tablespoon sunflower oil
- 1 tablespoon coconut sugar
- ¼ teaspoon vanilla
- ¼ teaspoon cinnamon
- ¼ teaspoon sea salt

Instructions:

1. Preheat the air fryer to 120°C.
2. Mix together the oats, maple syrup, sunflower oil, coconut sugar, vanilla, cinnamon, and sea salt in a medium bowl and stir to combine. Transfer the mixture to a baking pan.
3. Place the pan in the air fryer basket and bake for 40 minutes, or until the granola is mostly dry and lightly browned. Stir the granola four times during cooking.
4. Let the granola stand for 5 to 10 minutes before serving.

Bacon Eggs on the Go

Serves 1

Prep time: 5 minutes / Cook time: 15 minutes

Ingredients:

- 2 eggs
- 110 g bacon, cooked
- Salt and ground black pepper, to taste

Instructions:

1. Preheat the air fryer to 204°C. Put liners in a regular cupcake tin.
2. Crack an egg into each of the cups and add the bacon. Season with some pepper and salt.
3. Bake in the preheated air fryer for 15 minutes, or until the eggs are set. Serve warm.

White Bean–Oat Waffles

Serves 2

Prep time: 10 minutes / Cook time: 20 minutes

Ingredients:

- 1 large egg white

- 2 tablespoons finely ground flaxseed
- 120 ml water
- ¼ teaspoon salt
- 1 teaspoon vanilla extract
- 120 ml cannellini beans, drained and rinsed
- 1 teaspoon coconut oil
- 1 teaspoon liquid sweetener
- 120 ml old-fashioned rolled oats
- Extra-virgin olive oil cooking spray

Instructions:

1. In a blender, combine the egg white, flaxseed, water, salt, vanilla, cannellini beans, coconut oil, and sweetener. Blend on high for 90 seconds.
2. Add the oats. Blend for 1 minute more.
3. Preheat the waffle iron. The batter will thicken to the correct consistency while the waffle iron preheats.
4. Spray the heated waffle iron with cooking spray.
5. Add 180 ml batter. Close the waffle iron. Cook for 6 to 8 minutes, or until done. Repeated with the remaining batter.
6. Serve hot, with your favorite sugar-free topping.

Denver Omelette

Serves 1

Prep time: 5 minutes / Cook time: 8 minutes

Ingredients:

- 2 large eggs
- 60 ml unsweetened, unflavoured almond milk
- ¼ teaspoon fine sea salt
- ⅛ teaspoon ground black pepper
- 60 ml diced ham (omit for vegetarian)
- 60 ml diced green and red peppers
- 2 tablespoons diced spring onions, plus more for garnish
- 60 ml shredded Cheddar cheese (about 30 g) (omit for dairy-free)
- Quartered cherry tomatoes, for serving (optional)

Instructions:

1. Preheat the air fryer to 176°C. Grease a cake pan and set aside.
2. In a small bowl, use a fork to whisk together the eggs, almond milk, salt, and pepper. Add the ham, peppers, and spring onions. Pour the mixture into the greased pan. Add the cheese on top (if using).
3. Place the pan in the basket of the air fryer. Bake for 8 minutes, or until the eggs are cooked to your liking.
4. Loosen the omelette from the sides of the pan with a spatula and place it on a serving plate. Garnish with spring onions and serve with cherry tomatoes, if desired. Best served fresh.

Butternut Squash and Ricotta Frittata

Serves 2 to 3

Prep time: 10 minutes / Cook time: 33 minutes

Ingredients:

- 235 ml cubed (½-inch) butternut squash (160 g)
- 2 tablespoons olive oil
- Coarse or flaky salt and freshly ground black pepper, to taste
- 4 fresh sage leaves, thinly sliced
- 6 large eggs, lightly beaten
- 120 ml ricotta cheese
- Cayenne pepper

Instructions:

1. In a bowl, toss the squash with the olive oil and season with salt and black pepper until evenly coated. Sprinkle the sage on the bottom of a cake pan and place the squash on top. Place the pan in the air fryer and bake at 204°C for 10 minutes. Stir to incorporate the sage, then cook until the squash is tender and lightly caramelized at the edges, about 3 minutes more.
2. Pour the eggs over the squash, dollop the

ricotta all over, and sprinkle with cayenne. Bake at 150°C until the eggs are set and the frittata is golden brown on top, about 20 minutes. Remove the pan from the air fryer and cut the frittata into wedges to serve.

Parmesan Sausage Egg Muffins

Serves 4

Prep time: 5 minutes / Cook time: 20 minutes

Ingredients:
- 170 g Italian-seasoned sausage, sliced
- 6 eggs
- 30 ml double cream
- Salt and ground black pepper, to taste
- 85 g Parmesan cheese, grated

Instructions:
1. Preheat the air fryer to 176°C. Grease a muffin pan.
2. Put the sliced sausage in the muffin pan.
3. Beat the eggs with the cream in a bowl and season with salt and pepper.
4. Pour half of the mixture over the sausages in the pan.
5. Sprinkle with cheese and the remaining egg mixture.
6. Bake in the preheated air fryer for 20 minutes or until set.
7. Serve immediately.

Poached Eggs on Whole Grain Avocado Toast

Serves 4

Prep time: 5 minutes / Cook time: 7 minutes

Ingredients:
- Olive oil cooking spray
- 4 large eggs
- Salt
- Black pepper
- 4 pieces wholegrain bread
- 1 avocado
- Red pepper flakes (optional)

Instructions:
1. Preheat the air fryer to 160°C. Lightly coat the inside of four small oven-safe ramekins with olive oil cooking spray.
2. Crack one egg into each ramekin, and season with salt and black pepper.
3. Place the ramekins into the air fryer basket. Close and set the timer to 7 minutes.
4. While the eggs are cooking, toast the bread in a toaster.
5. Slice the avocado in half lengthwise, remove the pit, and scoop the flesh into a small bowl. Season with salt, black pepper, and red pepper flakes, if desired. Using a fork, smash the avocado lightly.
6. Spread a quarter of the smashed avocado evenly over each slice of toast.
7. Remove the eggs from the air fryer, and gently spoon one onto each slice of avocado toast before serving.

Potatoes Lyonnaise

Serves 4

Prep time: 10 minutes / Cook time: 31 minutes

Ingredients:
- 1 sweet/mild onion, sliced
- 1 teaspoon butter, melted
- 1 teaspoon brown sugar
- 2 large white potatoes (about 450 g in total), sliced ½-inch thick
- 1 tablespoon vegetable oil
- Salt and freshly ground black pepper, to taste

Instructions:
1. Preheat the air fryer to 188°C.
2. Toss the sliced onions, melted butter and brown sugar together in the air fryer basket. Air fry for 8 minutes, shaking the basket occasionally to help the onions cook evenly.

3. While the onions are cooking, bring a saucepan of salted water to a boil on the stovetop. Par-cook the potatoes in boiling water for 3 minutes. Drain the potatoes and pat them dry with a clean kitchen towel.
4. Add the potatoes to the onions in the air fryer basket and drizzle with vegetable oil. Toss to coat the potatoes with the oil and season with salt and freshly ground black pepper.
5. Increase the air fryer temperature to 204ºC and air fry for 20 minutes, tossing the vegetables a few times during the cooking time to help the potatoes brown evenly.
6. Season with salt and freshly ground black pepper and serve warm.

Asparagus and Bell Pepper Strata

Serves 4

Prep time: 10 minutes / Cook time: 14 to 20 minutes

Ingredients:
- 8 large asparagus spears, trimmed and cut into 2-inch pieces
- 80 ml shredded carrot
- 120 ml chopped red pepper
- 2 slices wholemeal bread, cut into ½-inch cubes
- 3 egg whites
- 1 egg
- 3 tablespoons 1% milk
- ½ teaspoon dried thyme

Instructions:
1. In a baking pan, combine the asparagus, carrot, red bell pepper, and 1 tablespoon of water. Bake in the air fryer at 166ºC for 3 to 5 minutes, or until crisp-tender. Drain well.
2. Add the bread cubes to the vegetables and gently toss.
3. In a medium bowl, whisk the egg whites, egg, milk, and thyme until frothy.
4. Pour the egg mixture into the pan. Bake for 11 to 15 minutes, or until the strata is slightly puffy

and set and the top starts to brown. Serve.

Mississippi Spice Muffins

Makes 12 muffins

Prep time: 15 minutes / Cook time: 13 minutes

Ingredients:
- 1 L plain flour
- 1 tablespoon ground cinnamon
- 2 teaspoons baking soda
- 2 teaspoons allspice
- 1 teaspoon ground cloves
- 1 teaspoon salt
- 235 ml (2 sticks) butter, room temperature
- 475 ml sugar
- 2 large eggs, lightly beaten
- 475 ml unsweetened applesauce
- 60 ml chopped pecans
- 1 to 2 tablespoons oil

Instructions:
1. In a large bowl, whisk the flour, cinnamon, baking soda, allspice, cloves, and salt until blended.
2. In another large bowl, combine the butter and sugar. Using an electric mixer, beat the mixture for 2 to 3 minutes until light and fluffy. Add the beaten eggs and stir until blended.
3. Add the flour mixture and applesauce, alternating between the two and blending after each addition. Stir in the pecans.
4. Preheat the air fryer to 164ºC. Spritz 12 silicone muffin cups with oil.
5. Pour the batter into the prepared muffin cups, filling each halfway. Place the muffins in the air fryer basket.
6. Air fry for 6 minutes. Shake the basket and air fry for 7 minutes more. The muffins are done when a toothpick inserted into the middle comes out clean.

Easy Sausage Pizza

Serves 4

Prep time: 10 minutes / Cook time: 6 minutes

Ingredients:

- 2 tablespoons ketchup
- 1 pitta bread
- 80 ml sausage meat
- 230 g Mozzarella cheese
- 1 teaspoon garlic powder
- 1 tablespoon olive oil

Instructions:

1. Preheat the air fryer to 172ºC.
2. Spread the ketchup over the pitta bread.
3. Top with the sausage meat and cheese. Sprinkle with the garlic powder and olive oil.
4. Put the pizza in the air fryer basket and bake for 6 minutes.
5. Serve warm.

Portobello Eggs Benedict

Serves 2

Prep time: 10 minutes / Cook time: 10 to 14 minutes

Ingredients:

- 1 tablespoon olive oil
- 2 cloves garlic, minced
- ¼ teaspoon dried thyme
- 2 portobello mushrooms, stems removed and gills scraped out
- 2 plum tomatoes, halved lengthwise
- Salt and freshly ground black pepper, to taste
- 2 large eggs
- 2 tablespoons grated Pecorino Romano cheese
- 1 tablespoon chopped fresh parsley, for garnish
- 1 teaspoon truffle oil (optional)

Instructions:

1. Preheat the air fryer to 204ºC.
2. In a small bowl, combine the olive oil, garlic,

and thyme. Brush the mixture over the mushrooms and tomatoes until thoroughly coated. Season to taste with salt and freshly ground black pepper.

3. Arrange the vegetables, cut side up, in the air fryer basket. Crack an egg into the center of each mushroom and sprinkle with cheese. Air fry for 10 to 14 minutes until the vegetables are tender and the whites are firm. When cool enough to handle, coarsely chop the tomatoes and place on top of the eggs. Scatter parsley on top and drizzle with truffle oil, if desired, just before serving.

Italian Egg Cups

Serves 4

Prep time: 5 minutes / Cook time: 10 minutes

Ingredients:

- Olive oil
- 235 ml marinara sauce
- 4 eggs
- 4 tablespoons shredded Mozzarella cheese
- 4 teaspoons grated Parmesan cheese
- Salt and freshly ground black pepper, to taste
- Chopped fresh basil, for garnish

Instructions:

1. Lightly spray 4 individual ramekins with olive oil.
2. Pour 60 ml marinara sauce into each ramekin.
3. Crack one egg into each ramekin on top of the marinara sauce.
4. Sprinkle 1 tablespoon of Mozzarella and 1 tablespoon of Parmesan on top of each egg. Season with salt and pepper.
5. Cover each ramekin with aluminum foil. Place two of the ramekins in the air fryer basket.
6. Air fry at 176ºC for 5 minutes and remove the aluminum foil. Air fry until the top is lightly browned and the egg white is cooked, another 2 to 4 minutes. If you prefer the yolk

to be firmer, cook for 3 to 5 more minutes.

7. Repeat with the remaining two ramekins. Garnish with basil and serve.

All-in-One Toast

Serves 1

Prep time: 10 minutes / Cook time: 10 minutes

Ingredients:

- 1 strip bacon, diced
- 1 slice 1-inch thick bread
- 1 egg
- Salt and freshly ground black pepper, to taste
- 60 ml grated Monterey Jack or Chedday cheese

Instructions:

1. Preheat the air fryer to 204°C.
2. Air fry the bacon for 3 minutes, shaking the basket once or twice while it cooks. Remove the bacon to a paper towel lined plate and set aside.
3. Use a sharp paring knife to score a large circle in the middle of the slice of bread, cutting halfway through, but not all the way through to the cutting board. Press down on the circle in the center of the bread slice to create an indentation.
4. Transfer the slice of bread, hole side up, to the air fryer basket. Crack the egg into the center of the bread, and season with salt and pepper.
5. Adjust the air fryer temperature to 192°C and air fry for 5 minutes. Sprinkle the grated cheese around the edges of the bread, leaving the center of the yolk uncovered, and top with the cooked bacon. Press the cheese and bacon into the bread lightly to help anchor it to the bread and prevent it from blowing around in the air fryer.
6. Air fry for one or two more minutes, just to melt the cheese and finish cooking the egg. Serve immediately.

Mexican Breakfast Pepper Rings

Serves 4

Prep time: 5 minutes / Cook time: 10 minutes

Ingredients:

- Olive oil
- 1 large red, yellow, or orange pepper, cut into four ¾-inch rings
- 4 eggs
- Salt and freshly ground black pepper, to taste
- 2 teaspoons salsa

Instructions:

1. Preheat the air fryer to 176°C. Lightly spray a baking pan with olive oil.
2. Place 2 bell pepper rings on the pan. Crack one egg into each bell pepper ring. Season with salt and black pepper.
3. Spoon ½ teaspoon of salsa on top of each egg.
4. Place the pan in the air fryer basket. Air fry until the yolk is slightly runny, 5 to 6 minutes or until the yolk is fully cooked, 8 to 10 minutes.
5. Repeat with the remaining 2 pepper rings. Serve hot.

Pancake for Two

Serves 2

Prep time: 5 minutes / Cook time: 30 minutes

Ingredients:

- 235 ml blanched finely ground almond flour
- 2 tablespoons granular erythritol
- 1 tablespoon salted butter, melted
- 1 large egg
- 80 ml unsweetened almond milk
- ½ teaspoon vanilla extract

Instructions:

1. In a large bowl, mix all ingredients together,

then pour half the batter into an ungreased round nonstick baking dish.

2. Place dish into air fryer basket. Adjust the temperature to 160ºC and bake for 15 minutes. The pancake will be golden brown on top and firm, and a toothpick inserted in the center will come out clean when done. Repeat with remaining batter.

3. Slice in half in dish and serve warm.

Super Easy Bacon Cups

Serves 2

Prep time: 5 minutes / Cook time: 20 minutes

Ingredients:

- 3 slices bacon, cooked, sliced in half
- 2 slices ham
- 1 slice tomato
- 2 eggs
- 2 teaspoons grated Parmesan cheese
- Salt and ground black pepper, to taste

Instructions:

1. Preheat the air fryer to 192ºC. Line 2 greased muffin tins with 3 half-strips of bacon 2. Put one slice of ham and half slice of tomato in each muffin tin on top of the bacon 3. Crack one egg on top of the tomato in each muffin tin and sprinkle each with half a teaspoon of grated Parmesan cheese. Sprinkle with salt and ground black pepper, if desired.

4. Bake in the preheated air fryer for 20 minutes. Remove from the air fryer and let cool.

5. Serve warm.

Pizza Eggs

Serves 2

Prep time: 5 minutes / Cook time: 10 minutes

Ingredients:

- 235 ml shredded Mozzarella cheese

- 7 slices pepperoni, chopped
- 1 large egg, whisked
- ¼ teaspoon dried oregano
- ¼ teaspoon dried parsley
- ¼ teaspoon garlic powder
- ¼ teaspoon salt

Instructions:

1. Place Mozzarella in a single layer on the bottom of an ungreased round nonstick baking dish. Scatter pepperoni over cheese, then pour egg evenly around baking dish.

2. Sprinkle with remaining ingredients and place into air fryer basket. Adjust the temperature to 166ºC and bake for 10 minutes. When cheese is brown and egg is set, dish will be done.

3. Let cool in dish 5 minutes before serving.

Chimichanga Breakfast Burrito

Serves 2

Prep time: 10 minutes / Cook time: 10 minutes

Ingredients:

- 2 large (10- to 12-inch) flour tortillas
- 120 ml canned refried beans (pinto or black work equally well)
- 4 large eggs, cooked scrambled
- 4 corn tortilla chips, crushed
- 120 ml grated chili cheese
- 12 pickled jalapeño slices
- 1 tablespoon vegetable oil
- Guacamole, salsa, and sour cream, for serving (optional)

Instructions:

1. Place the tortillas on a work surface and divide the refried beans between them, spreading them in a rough rectangle in the center of the tortillas. Top the beans with the scrambled eggs, crushed chips, cheese, and

jalapeños. Fold one side over the fillings, then fold in each short side and roll up the rest of the way like a burrito.

2. Brush the outside of the burritos with the oil, then transfer to the air fryer, seam-side down. Air fry at 176ºC until the tortillas are browned and crisp and the filling is warm throughout, about 10 minutes.

3. Transfer the chimichangas to plates and serve warm with guacamole, salsa, and sour cream, if you like.

Pancake Cake

Serves 4

Prep time: 10 minutes / Cook time: 7 minutes

Ingredients:

* 120 ml blanched finely ground almond flour
* 60 ml powdered erythritol
* ½ teaspoon baking powder
* 2 tablespoons unsalted butter, softened
* 1 large egg
* ½ teaspoon unflavoured gelatin
* ½ teaspoon vanilla extract
* ½ teaspoon ground cinnamon

Instructions:

1. In a large bowl, mix almond flour, erythritol, and baking powder. Add butter, egg, gelatin, vanilla, and cinnamon. Pour into a round baking pan.
2. Place pan into the air fryer basket.
3. Adjust the temperature to 150ºC and set the timer for 7 minutes.
4. When the cake is completely cooked, a toothpick will come out clean. Cut cake into four and serve.

Air Fryer Donuts

Serves 6

Prep time: 15 minutes / Cook Time: 10 minutes

Ingredients:

* 2 cups (250g) all-purpose flour
* ½ cup (100g) granulated sugar
* 2 tsp (10g) baking powder
* ½ tsp (3g) salt
* ¾ cup (180ml) milk
* 2 large eggs
* 2 tbsp (28g) unsalted butter, melted
* 1 tsp (5ml) vanilla extract
* Cooking spray
* ¼ cup (30g) powdered sugar, for dusting

Instructions:

1. Preheat your air fryer to 180°C.
2. In a mixing bowl, whisk together the flour, granulated sugar, baking powder, and salt.
3. In a separate bowl, whisk together the milk, eggs, melted butter, and vanilla extract until well combined.
4. Pour the wet ingredients into the dry ingredients and mix until just combined. Do not overmix.
5. Lightly coat the air fryer basket with cooking spray.
6. Scoop the donut batter into a piping bag or a ziplock bag with one corner cut off.
7. Pipe the batter into the air fryer basket, forming six donuts.
8. Air fry the donuts for 5 minutes.
9. Flip the donuts over and air fry for another 3-5 minutes or until golden brown and cooked through.
10. Remove the donuts from the air fryer basket and allow them to cool slightly on a wire rack.
11. Dust the powdered sugar over the donuts and serve.

Coconut Chicken Tenders

Serves 4

Prep time: 10 minutes / Cook time: 12 minutes

Ingredients:

- Oil, for spraying
- 2 large eggs
- 60 ml milk
- 1 tablespoon hot sauce
- 350 ml sweetened flaked or desiccated coconut
- 180 ml panko breadcrumbs
- 1 teaspoon salt
- ½ teaspoon freshly ground black pepper
- 450 g chicken tenders

Instructions:

1. Line the air fryer basket with parchment and spray lightly with oil.
2. In a small bowl, whisk together the eggs, milk, and hot sauce.
3. In a shallow dish, mix together the coconut, breadcrumbs, salt, and black pepper.
4. Coat the chicken in the egg mix, then dredge in the coconut mixture until evenly coated.
5. Place the chicken in the prepared basket and spray liberally with oil.
6. Air fry at 204°C for 6 minutes, flip, spray with more oil, and cook for another 6 minutes, or until the internal temperature reaches 74°C.

Air Fryer Biscuits & Gravy

Serves: 4

Prep Time: 10 minutes/Cook Time: 15 minutes

Ingredients:

For the Biscuits:

- 2 cups (250g) all-purpose flour
- 1 tbsp (12g) baking powder
- ½ tsp (2g) salt
- ½ cup (113g) unsalted butter, cold and cut into small pieces
- ¾ cup (177ml) buttermilk

For the Gravy:

- 1 lb (454g) ground pork sausage
- 3 tbsp (24g) all-purpose flour
- 2 cups (473ml) whole milk
- Salt and pepper, to taste

Instructions:

1. Preheat your air fryer to 200°C.
2. In a large mixing bowl, whisk together the flour, baking powder, and salt.
3. Add the cold butter pieces to the flour mixture and use a pastry cutter or your fingers to cut the butter into the flour mixture until the mixture resembles coarse crumbs.
4. Gradually add the buttermilk to the mixture and stir until the dough forms a ball.
5. Place the dough on a floured surface and knead it lightly.
6. Roll out the dough to ½ inch (1.3cm) thickness and cut out biscuits using a biscuit cutter.
7. Place the biscuits in the air fryer basket in a single layer and cook for 8-10 minutes or until golden brown.
8. While the biscuits are cooking, heat a large skillet over medium-high heat and cook the sausage until browned, breaking it up into small pieces with a spatula.
9. Sprinkle the flour over the sausage and stir to combine.
10. Gradually pour in the milk, stirring constantly, until the mixture thickens.
11. Season the gravy with salt and pepper to taste.
12. Serve the biscuits hot from the air fryer and top them with the sausage gravy.

Scallops with Green Vegetables

Serves 4

Prep time: 15 minutes / Cook time: 8 to 11 minutes

Ingredients:

- 235 ml green beans
- 235 ml frozen peas
- 235 ml frozen chopped broccoli
- 2 teaspoons olive oil
- ½ teaspoon dried basil
- ½ teaspoon dried oregano
- 340 g sea scallops

Instructions:

1. In a large bowl, toss the green beans, peas, and broccoli with the olive oil. Place in the air fryer basket.
2. Air fry at 204°C for 4 to 6 minutes, or until the vegetables are crisp-tender.
3. Remove the vegetables from the air fryer basket and sprinkle with the herbs.
4. Set aside. In the air fryer basket, put the scallops and air fry for 4 to 5 minutes, or until the scallops are firm and reach an internal temperature of just 64°C on a meat thermometer.
5. Toss scallops with the vegetables and serve immediately.

Cheesy Roasted Sweet Potatoes

Serves 4

Prep time: 7 minutes / Cook time: 18 to 23 minutes

Ingredients:

- 2 large sweet potatoes, peeled and sliced
- 1 teaspoon olive oil
- 1 tablespoon white balsamic vinegar
- 1 teaspoon dried thyme
- 60 ml grated Parmesan cheese

Instructions:

1. In a large bowl, drizzle the sweet potato slices with the olive oil and toss.
2. Sprinkle with the balsamic vinegar and thyme and toss again.
3. Sprinkle the potatoes with the Parmesan cheese and toss to coat.
4. Roast the slices, in batches, in the air fryer basket at 204°C for 18 to 23 minutes, tossing the sweet potato slices in the basket once during cooking, until tender.
5. Repeat with the remaining sweet potato slices.
6. Serve immediately.

Churro Bites

Makes 36 bites

Prep time: 5 minutes / Cook time: 6 minutes

Ingredients:

- Oil, for spraying
- 1 (500 g) package frozen puffed pastry, thawed
- 235 ml granulated sugar
- 1 tablespoon ground cinnamon
- 120 ml icing sugar
- 1 tablespoon milk

Instructions:

1. Preheat the air fryer to 204°C.
2. Line the air fryer basket with parchment and spray lightly with oil.
3. Unfold the puff pastry onto a clean work surface.
4. Using a sharp knife, cut the dough into 36 bite-size pieces.
5. Place the dough pieces in one layer in the prepared basket, taking care not to let the pieces touch or overlap.
6. Cook for 3 minutes, flip, and cook for another 3 minutes, or until puffed and golden.
7. In a small bowl, mix together the granulated sugar and cinnamon.

8. In another small bowl, whisk together the icing sugar and milk.
9. Dredge the bites in the cinnamon-sugar mixture until evenly coated. Serve with the icing on the side for dipping.

Fish and Vegetable Tacos

Serves 4

Prep time: 15 minutes / Cook time: 9 to 12 minutes

Ingredients:
- 450 g white fish fillets, such as sole or cod
- 2 teaspoons olive oil
- 3 tablespoons freshly squeezed lemon juice, divided
- 350 ml chopped red cabbage
- 1 large carrot, grated
- 120 ml low-salt salsa
- 80 ml low-fat Greek yoghurt
- 4 soft low-salt wholemeal tortillas

Instructions:
1. Brush the fish with the olive oil and sprinkle with 1 tablespoon of lemon juice.
2. Air fry in the air fryer basket at 200°C for 9 to 12 minutes, or until the fish just flakes when tested with a fork.
3. Meanwhile, in a medium bowl, stir together the remaining 2 tablespoons of lemon juice, the red cabbage, carrot, salsa, and yoghurt.
4. When the fish is cooked, remove it from the air fryer basket and break it up into large pieces.
5. Offer the fish, tortillas, and the cabbage mixture, and let each person assemble a taco.

Cheesy Potato Patties

Serves 8

Prep time: 5 minutes / Cook time: 10 minutes

Ingredients:
- 900 g white potatoes
- 120 ml finely chopped spring onions
- ½ teaspoon freshly ground black pepper, or more to taste
- 1 tablespoon fine sea salt
- ½ teaspoon hot paprika
- 475 ml shredded Colby or Monterey Jack cheese
- 60 ml rapeseed oil
- 235 ml crushed crackers

Instructions:
1. Preheat the air fryer to 182°C.
2. Boil the potatoes until soft.
3. Dry them off and peel them before mashing thoroughly, leaving no lumps.
4. Combine the mashed potatoes with spring onions, pepper, salt, paprika, and cheese.
5. Mould the mixture into balls with your hands and press with your palm to flatten them into patties.
6. In a shallow dish, combine the rapeseed oil and crushed crackers. Coat the patties in the crumb mixture.
7. Bake the patties for about 10 minutes, in multiple batches if necessary. Serve hot.

Traditional Queso Fundido

Serves 4

Prep time: 10 minutes / Cook time: 25 minutes

Ingredients:

- 110 g fresh Mexican (or Spanish if unavailable) chorizo, casings removed
- 1 medium onion, chopped
- 3 cloves garlic, minced
- 235 ml chopped tomato
- 2 jalapeños, deseeded and diced
- 2 teaspoons ground cumin
- 475 ml shredded Oaxaca or Mozzarella cheese
- 120 ml half-and-half (60 ml whole milk and 60 ml cream combined)
- Celery sticks or tortilla chips, for serving

Instructions:

1. Preheat the air fryer to 204ºC.
2. In a baking pan, combine the chorizo, onion, garlic, tomato, jalapeños, and cumin.
3. Stir to combine. Place the pan in the air fryer basket.
4. Air fry for 15 minutes, or until the sausage is cooked, stirring halfway through the cooking time to break up the sausage.
5. Add the cheese and half-and-half; stir to combine.
6. Air fry for 10 minutes, or until the cheese has melted.
7. Serve with celery sticks or tortilla chips.

Sweet Corn and Carrot Fritters

Serves 4

Prep time: 10 minutes / Cook time: 8 to 11 minutes

Instructions:

1. Preheat the air fryer to 176ºC.
2. Place the grated carrot in a colander and press down to squeeze out any excess moisture.
3. Dry it with a paper towel. Combine the carrots with the remaining ingredients.
4. Mould 1 tablespoon of the mixture into a ball and press it down with your hand or a spoon to flatten it.
5. Repeat until the rest of the mixture is used up.
6. Spritz the balls with cooking spray.
7. Arrange in the air fryer basket, taking care not to overlap any balls.
8. Bake for 8 to 11 minutes, or until they're firm. Serve warm.

Easy Devils on Horseback

Serves 12

Prep time: 5 minutes / Cook time: 7 minutes

Ingredients:

- 24 small pitted prunes (128 g)
- 60 ml crumbled blue cheese, divided
- 8 slices centre-cut bacon, cut crosswise into thirds

Instructions:

1. Preheat the air fryer to 204ºC.
2. Halve the prunes lengthwise, but don't cut them all the way through.
3. Place ½ teaspoon of cheese in the centre of each prune.
4. Wrap a piece of bacon around each prune and secure the bacon with a toothpick.

5. Working in batches, arrange a single layer of the prunes in the air fryer basket.
6. Air fry for about 7 minutes, flipping halfway, until the bacon is cooked through and crisp.
7. Let cool slightly and serve warm.

Baked Halloumi with Greek Salsa

Prep timeBaked Halloumi with Greek Salsa

Ingredients:
Salsa:
- 1 small shallot, finely diced
- 3 garlic cloves, minced
- 2 tablespoons fresh lemon juice
- 2 tablespoons extra-virgin olive oil
- 1 teaspoon freshly cracked black pepper
- Pinch of rock salt
- 120 ml finely diced English cucumber
- 1 plum tomato, deseeded and finely diced
- 2 teaspoons chopped fresh parsley
- 1 teaspoon snipped fresh dill
- 1 teaspoon snipped fresh oregano

Cheese:
- 227 g Halloumi cheese, sliced into ½-inch-thick pieces
- 1 tablespoon extra-virgin olive oil

Instructions:
1. Preheat the air fryer to 192ºC.
2. For the salsa: Combine the shallot, garlic, lemon juice, olive oil, pepper, and salt in a medium bowl. Add the cucumber, tomato, parsley, dill, and oregano. Toss gently to combine; set aside.
3. For the cheese: Place the cheese slices in a medium bowl. Drizzle with the olive oil. Toss gently to coat. Arrange the cheese in a single layer in the air fryer basket. Bake for 6 minutes. Divide the cheese among four serving plates.
4. Top with the salsa and serve immediately.

Buttery Sweet Potatoes

Serves 4

Prep time: 5 minutes / Cook time: 10 minutes

Ingredients:
- 2 tablespoons butter, melted
- 1 tablespoon light brown sugar
- 2 sweet potatoes, peeled and cut into ½-inch cubes
- Cooking spray

Instructions:
1. Preheat the air fryer to 204ºC.
2. Line the air fryer basket with parchment paper.
3. In a medium bowl, stir together the melted butter and brown sugar until blended.
4. Toss the sweet potatoes in the butter mixture until coated.
5. Place the sweet potatoes on the parchment and spritz with oil.
6. Air fry for 5 minutes.
7. Shake the basket, spritz the sweet potatoes with oil, and air fry for 5 minutes more until they're soft enough to cut with a fork.
8. Serve immediately.

Herb-Roasted Veggies

Serves 4

Prep time: 10 minutes / Cook time: 14 to 18 minutes

Ingredients:
- 1 red pepper, sliced
- 1 (230 g) package sliced mushrooms
- 235 ml green beans, cut into 2-inch pieces
- 80 ml diced red onion
- 3 garlic cloves, sliced
- 1 teaspoon olive oil
- ½ teaspoon dried basil
- ½ teaspoon dried tarragon

Instructions:

1. Preheat the air fryer to 176°C.
2. In a medium bowl, mix the red pepper, mushrooms, green beans, red onion, and garlic.
3. Drizzle with the olive oil. Toss to coat.
4. Add the herbs and toss again.
5. Place the vegetables in the air fryer basket. Roast for 14 to 18 minutes, or until tender.
6. Serve immediately.

Cheesy Baked Grits

Serves 6

Prep time: 10 minutes / Cook time: 12 minutes

Ingredients:

- 180 ml hot water
- 2 (28 g) packages instant grits
- 1 large egg, beaten
- 1 tablespoon butter, melted
- 2 cloves garlic, minced
- ½ to 1 teaspoon red pepper flakes
- 235 ml shredded Cheddar cheese or jalapeño Jack cheese

Instructions:

1. Preheat the air fryer to 204°C.
2. In a baking pan, combine the water, grits, egg, butter, garlic, and red pepper flakes. Stir until well combined.
3. Stir in the shredded cheese.
4. Place the pan in the air fryer basket and air fry for 12 minutes, or until the grits have cooked through and a knife inserted near the centre comes out clean.
5. Let stand for 5 minutes before serving.

Crunchy Fried Okra

Serves 4

Prep time: 5 minutes / Cook time: 8 to 10 minutes

Ingredients:

- 235 ml self-raising yellow cornmeal (alternatively add 1 tablespoon baking powder to cornmeal)
- 1 teaspoon Italian-style seasoning
- 1 teaspoon paprika
- 1 teaspoon salt
- ½ teaspoon freshly ground black pepper
- 2 large eggs, beaten
- 475 ml okra slices
- Cooking spray

Instructions:

1. Preheat the air fryer to 204°C.
2. Line the air fryer basket with parchment paper.
3. In a shallow bowl, whisk the cornmeal, Italian-style seasoning, paprika, salt, and pepper until blended.
4. Place the beaten eggs in a second shallow bowl.
5. Add the okra to the beaten egg and stir to coat.
6. Add the egg and okra mixture to the cornmeal mixture and stir until coated.
7. Place the okra on the parchment and spritz it with oil.
8. Air fry for 4 minutes. Shake the basket, spritz the okra with oil, and air fry for 4 to 6 minutes more until lightly browned and crispy.
9. Serve immediately.

Peppery Brown Rice Fritters

Serves 4

Prep time: 10 minutes / Cook time: 8 to 10 minutes

Ingredients:

- 1 (284 g) bag frozen cooked brown rice, thawed
- 1 egg
- 3 tablespoons brown rice flour
- 80 ml finely grated carrots
- 80 ml minced red pepper
- 2 tablespoons minced fresh basil
- 3 tablespoons grated Parmesan cheese
- 2 teaspoons olive oil

Instructions:

1. Preheat the air fryer to 192°C.
2. In a small bowl, combine the thawed rice, egg, and flour and mix to blend.
3. Stir in the carrots, pepper, basil, and Parmesan cheese. Form the mixture into 8 fritters and drizzle with the olive oil.
4. Put the fritters carefully into the air fryer basket. Air fry for 8 to 10 minutes, or until the fritters are golden brown and cooked through. Serve immediately.

Air Fryer Spiced Chickpeas

Serves: 4

Prep Time: 5 minutes/Cook Time: 15 minutes

Ingredients:

- 1 can (400g) chickpeas, drained and rinsed
- 1 tbsp (15ml) olive oil
- 1 tsp (5g) ground cumin
- 1 tsp (5g) smoked paprika
- ½ tsp (2. 5g) garlic powder
- ½ tsp (2. 5g) onion powder
- ½ tsp (2. 5g) salt
- ¼ tsp (1. 25g) black pepper

Instructions:

1. Preheat your air fryer to 180°C.
2. In a mixing bowl, add chickpeas, olive oil, cumin, smoked paprika, garlic powder, onion powder, salt, and black pepper.
3. Toss the chickpeas to evenly coat them with the spices.
4. Place the chickpeas in the air fryer basket in a single layer.
5. Cook for 15 minutes or until the chickpeas are crispy and golden brown, shaking the basket halfway through the cooking time.
6. Once the chickpeas are done, remove them from the air fryer and let them cool for a few minutes before serving.
7. Serve as a snack or a topping for salads.

CHAPTER 3 FISH AND SEAFOOD

Almond-Crusted Fish

Serves 4

Prep time: 15 minutes / Cook time: 10 minutes

Ingredients:
- 4 firm white fish fillets, 110g each
- 45 g breadcrumbs
- 20 g slivered almonds, crushed
- 2 tablespoons lemon juice
- ⅛ teaspoon cayenne
- Salt and pepper, to taste
- 940 g plain flour
- 1 egg, beaten with 1 tablespoon water
- Olive or vegetable oil for misting or cooking spray

Instructions:
1. Split fish fillets lengthwise down the center to create 8 pieces.
2. Mix breadcrumbs and almonds together and set aside.
3. Mix the lemon juice and cayenne together. Brush on all sides of fish.
4. Season fish to taste with salt and pepper.
5. Place the flour on a sheet of wax paper.
6. Roll fillets in flour, dip in egg wash, and roll in the crumb mixture.
7. Mist both sides of fish with oil or cooking spray.
8. Spray the air fryer basket and lay fillets inside.
9. Roast at 200ºC for 5 minutes, turn fish over, and cook for an additional 5 minutes or until fish is done and flakes easily.

Panko-Crusted Fish Sticks

Serves 4

Prep time: 10 minutes / Cook time: 15 minutes

Ingredients:
Tartar Sauce:
- 470 ml mayonnaise
- 2 tablespoons dill pickle relish
- 1 tablespoon dried minced onions

Fish Sticks:
- Olive or vegetable oil, for spraying
- 455 g tilapia fillets
- 75 g plain flour
- 120 g panko bread crumbs
- 2 tablespoons Creole seasoning
- 2 teaspoons garlic granules
- 1 teaspoon onion powder
- ½ teaspoon salt
- ¼ teaspoon freshly ground black pepper
- 1 large egg

Instructions:
1. Make the Tartar Sauce: 1. In a small bowl, whisk together the mayonnaise, pickle relish, and onions. Cover with plastic wrap and refrigerate until ready to serve. You can make this sauce ahead of time; the flavors will intensify as it chills. Make the Fish Sticks: 2. Preheat the air fryer to 176ºC. Line the air fryer basket with baking paper and spray lightly with oil.
3. Cut the fillets into equal-size sticks and place them in a zip-top plastic bag.
4. Add the flour to the bag, seal, and shake well until evenly coated.
5. In a shallow bowl, mix together the bread crumbs, Creole seasoning, garlic, onion powder, salt, and black pepper.

6. In a small bowl, whisk the egg.

7. Dip the fish sticks in the egg, then dredge in the bread crumb mixture until completely coated.

8. Place the fish sticks in the prepared basket. You may need to work in batches, depending on the size of your air fryer. Do not overcrowd. Spray lightly with oil.

9. Cook for 12 to 15 minutes, or until browned and cooked through. Serve with the tartar sauce.

Confetti Salmon Burgers

Serves 4

Prep time: 10 minutes / Cook time: 12 minutes

Ingredients:

- 400 g cooked fresh or canned salmon, flaked with a fork
- 40 g minced spring onions, white and light green parts only
- 40 g minced red bell pepper
- 40 g minced celery
- 2 small lemons
- 1 teaspoon crab boil seasoning such as Old Bay
- ½ teaspoon kosher or coarse sea salt
- ½ teaspoon black pepper
- 1 egg, beaten
- 30 g fresh bread crumbs
- Vegetable oil, for spraying

Instructions:

1. In a large bowl, combine the salmon, vegetables, the zest and juice of 1 of the lemons, crab boil seasoning, salt, and pepper. Add the egg and bread crumbs and stir to combine. Form the mixture into 4 patties weighing approximately 140 g each. Chill until firm, about 15 minutes.

2. Preheat the air fryer to 204°C.

3. Spray the salmon patties with oil on all sides and spray the air fryer basket to prevent sticking. Air fry for 12 minutes, flipping halfway through, until the burgers are browned and cooked through. Cut the remaining lemon into 4 wedges and serve with the burgers.

chilli Lime Prawns

Serves 4

Prep time: 5 minutes / Cook time: 5 minutes

Ingredients:

- 455 g medium prawns, peeled and deveined
- 1 tablespoon salted butter, melted
- 2 teaspoons chilli powder
- ¼ teaspoon garlic powder
- ¼ teaspoon salt
- ¼ teaspoon ground black pepper
- ½ small lime, zested and juiced, divided

Instructions:

1. In a medium bowl, toss prawns with butter, then sprinkle with chilli powder, garlic powder, salt, pepper, and lime zest.

2. Place prawns into ungreased air fryer basket. Adjust the temperature to 204°C and air fry for 5 minutes. Prawns will be firm and form a "C" shape when done.

3. Transfer prawns to a large serving dish and drizzle with lime juice. Serve warm.

Tandoori-Spiced Salmon and Potatoes

Serves 2

Prep time: 10 minutes / Cook time: 28 minutes

Ingredients:

- 455 g Fingerling or new potatoes
- 2 tablespoons vegetable oil, divided

- Kosher or coarse sea salt and freshly ground black pepper, to taste
- 1 teaspoon ground turmeric
- 1 teaspoon ground cumin
- 1 teaspoon ground ginger
- ½ teaspoon smoked paprika
- ¼ teaspoon cayenne pepper
- 2 (170 g) skin-on salmon fillets

Instructions:

1. Preheat the air fryer to 192°C.
2. In a bowl, toss the potatoes with 1 tablespoon of the oil until evenly coated. Season with salt and pepper. Transfer the potatoes to the air fryer and air fry for 20 minutes.
3. Meanwhile, in a bowl, combine the remaining 1 tablespoon oil, the turmeric, cumin, ginger, paprika, and cayenne. Add the salmon fillets and turn in the spice mixture until fully coated all over.
4. After the potatoes have cooked for 20 minutes, place the salmon fillets, skin-side up, on top of the potatoes, and continue cooking until the potatoes are tender, the salmon is cooked, and the salmon skin is slightly crisp.
5. Transfer the salmon fillets to two plates and serve with the potatoes while both are warm.

Pesto Prawns with Wild Rice Pilaf

Serves 4

Prep time: 5 minutes / Cook time: 5 minutes

Ingredients:

- 455 g medium prawns, peeled and deveined
- 60 g pesto sauce
- 1 lemon, sliced
- 390 g cooked wild rice pilaf

Instructions:

1. Preheat the air fryer to 182°C.
2. In a medium bowl, toss the prawns with the pesto sauce until well coated.
3. Place the prawns in a single layer in the air fryer basket. Put the lemon slices over the prawns and roast for 5 minutes.
4. Remove the lemons and discard. Serve a quarter of the prawns over 100 g wild rice with some favorite steamed vegetables.

Dukkah-Crusted Halibut

Serves 2

Prep time: 15 minutes / Cook time: 17 minutes

Ingredients:

Dukkah:
- 1 tablespoon coriander seeds
- 1 tablespoon sesame seeds
- 1½ teaspoons cumin seeds
- 50 g roasted mixed nuts
- ¼ teaspoon kosher or coarse sea salt
- ¼ teaspoon black pepper

Fish:
- 2 halibut fillets, 140 g each
- 2 tablespoons mayonnaise
- Vegetable oil spray
- Lemon wedges, for serving

Instructions:

1. For the Dukkah: Combine the coriander, sesame seeds, and cumin in a small baking pan. Place the pan in the air fryer basket. Set the air fryer to 204°C for 5 minutes. Toward the end of the cooking time, you will hear the seeds popping. Transfer to a plate and let cool for 5 minutes.
2. Transfer the toasted seeds to a food processor or spice grinder and add the mixed nuts.

Pulse until coarsely chopped. Add the salt and pepper and stir well.

3. For the fish: Spread each fillet with 1 tablespoon of the mayonnaise. Press a heaping tablespoon of the Dukkah into the mayonnaise on each fillet, pressing lightly to adhere.

4. Spray the air fryer basket with vegetable oil spray. Place the fish in the basket. Cook for 12 minutes, or until the fish flakes easily with a fork.

5. Serve the fish with lemon wedges.

Crustless Prawn Quiche

Serves 2

Prep time: 15 minutes / Cook time: 20 minutes

Ingredients:

- Vegetable oil
- 4 large eggs
- 120 ml single cream
- 110 g raw prawns, chopped
- 120 g shredded Parmesan or Swiss cheese
- 235 g chopped spring onions
- 1 teaspoon sweet smoked paprika
- 1 teaspoon Herbes de Provence
- 1 teaspoon black pepper
- ½ to 1 teaspoon kosher or coarse sea salt

Instructions:

1. Generously grease a baking pan with vegetable oil. (Be sure to grease the pan well, the proteins in eggs stick something fierce. Alternatively, line the bottom of the pan with baking paper cut to fit and spray the baking paper and sides of the pan generously with vegetable oil spray.)

2. In a large bowl, beat together the eggs and single cream. Add the prawns, 90 g of the cheese, the scallions, paprika, Herbes de Provence, pepper, and salt. Stir with a fork

to thoroughly combine. Pour the egg mixture into the prepared pan.

3. Place the pan in the air fryer basket. Set the air fryer to 150°C for 20 minutes. After 17 minutes, sprinkle the remaining 30 g cheese on top and cook for the remaining 3 minutes, or until the cheese has melted, the eggs are set, and a toothpick inserted into the center comes out clean.

4. Serve the quiche warm or at room temperature.

Creamy Haddock

Serves 4

Prep time: 10 minutes / Cook time: 8 minutes

Ingredients:

- 455 g haddock fillet
- 1 teaspoon cayenne pepper
- 1 teaspoon salt
- 1 teaspoon coconut oil
- 120 ml heavy cream

Instructions:

1. Grease a baking pan with coconut oil.

2. Then put haddock fillet inside and sprinkle it with cayenne pepper, salt, and heavy cream. Put the baking pan in the air fryer basket and cook at 192°C for 8 minutes.

Catfish Bites

Serves 4

Prep time: 15 minutes / Cook time: 20 minutes

Ingredients:

- Olive or vegetable oil, for spraying
- 455 g catfish fillets, cut into 2-inch pieces
- 235 ml buttermilk
- 70 g cornmeal
- 30 g plain flour
- 2 teaspoons Creole seasoning
- 120 ml yellow mustard

Instructions:

1. Line the air fryer basket with baking paper and spray lightly with oil.
2. Place the catfish pieces and buttermilk in a zip-top plastic bag, seal, and refrigerate for about 10 minutes.
3. In a shallow bowl, mix together the cornmeal, flour, and Creole seasoning.
4. Remove the catfish from the bag and pat dry with a paper towel.
5. Spread the mustard on all sides of the catfish, then dip them in the cornmeal mixture until evenly coated.
6. Place the catfish in the prepared basket. You may need to work in batches, depending on the size of your air fryer. Spray lightly with oil.
7. Air fry at 204°C for 10 minutes, flip carefully, spray with oil, and cook for another 10 minutes. Serve immediately.

Parmesan Fish Fillets

Serves 4

Prep time: 8 minutes / Cook time: 17 minutes

Ingredients:

- 50 g grated Parmesan cheese
- ½ teaspoon fennel seed
- ½ teaspoon tarragon
- ⅓ teaspoon mixed peppercorns
- 2 eggs, beaten
- 4 (110 g) fish fillets, halved
- 2 tablespoons dry white wine
- 1 teaspoon seasoned salt

Instructions:

1. Preheat the air fryer to 174°C.
2. Place the grated Parmesan cheese, fennel seed, tarragon, and mixed peppercorns in a food processor and pulse for about 20 seconds until well combined. Transfer the cheese mixture to a shallow dish.
3. Place the beaten eggs in another shallow dish.
4. Drizzle the dry white wine over the top of fish fillets. Dredge each fillet in the beaten eggs on both sides, shaking off any excess, then roll them in the cheese mixture until fully coated. Season with the salt.
5. Arrange the fillets in the air fryer basket and air fry for about 17 minutes, or until the fish is cooked through and no longer translucent. Flip the fillets once halfway through the cooking time.
6. Cool for 5 minutes before serving.

Salmon on Bed of Fennel and Carrot

Serves 2

Prep time: 15 minutes / Cook time: 13 to 14 minutes

Ingredients:

- 1 fennel bulb, thinly sliced
- 1 large carrot, peeled and sliced
- 1 small onion, thinly sliced
- 60 ml low-fat sour cream
- ¼ teaspoon coarsely ground pepper
- 2 salmon fillets, 140 g each

Instructions:

1. Combine the fennel, carrot, and onion in a bowl and toss.
2. Put the vegetable mixture into a baking pan. Roast in the air fryer at 204°C for 4 minutes or until the vegetables are crisp-tender.
3. Remove the pan from the air fryer. Stir in the sour cream and sprinkle the vegetables with the pepper.
4. Top with the salmon fillets.
5. Return the pan to the air fryer. Roast for another 9 to 10 minutes or until the salmon just barely flakes when tested with a fork.

Bang Bang Prawns

Serves 4

Prep time: 15 minutes / Cook time: 14 minutes

Ingredients:

Sauce:
- 115 g mayonnaise
- 60 ml sweet chilli sauce
- 2 to 4 tablespoons Sriracha
- 1 teaspoon minced fresh ginger

Prawns:
- 455 g jumbo raw prawns (21 to 25 count), peeled and deveined
- 2 tablespoons cornflour or rice flour
- ½ teaspoon kosher or coarse sea salt
- Vegetable oil spray

Instructions:

1. For the sauce: In a large bowl, combine the mayonnaise, chilli sauce, Sriracha, and ginger. Stir until well combined. Remove half of the sauce to serve as a dipping sauce.
2. For the prawns: Place the prawns in a medium bowl. Sprinkle the cornflour and salt over the prawns and toss until well coated.
3. Place the prawns in the air fryer basket in a single layer. (If they won't fit in a single layer, set a rack or trivet on top of the bottom layer of prawns and place the rest of the prawns on the rack.) Spray generously with vegetable oil spray. Set the air fryer to 176ºC for 10 minutes, turning and spraying with additional oil spray halfway through the cooking time.
4. Remove the prawns and toss in the bowl with half of the sauce. Place the prawns back in the air fryer basket. Cook for an additional 4 to 5 minutes, or until the sauce has formed a glaze.
5. Serve the hot prawns with the reserved sauce for dipping.

Golden Beer-Battered Cod

Serves 4

Prep time: 5 minutes / Cook time: 15 minutes

Ingredients:

- 2 eggs
- 240 ml malty beer
- 120 g plain flour
- 60 g cornflour
- 1 teaspoon garlic powder
- Salt and pepper, to taste
- 4 cod fillets, 110 g each
- Cooking spray

Instructions:

1. Preheat the air fryer to 204ºC.
2. In a shallow bowl, beat together the eggs with the beer. In another shallow bowl, thoroughly combine the flour and cornflour. Sprinkle with the garlic powder, salt, and pepper.
3. Dredge each cod fillet in the flour mixture, then in the egg mixture. Dip each piece of fish in the flour mixture a second time.
4. Spritz the air fryer basket with cooking spray. Arrange the cod fillets in the basket in a single layer.
5. Air fry in batches for 15 minutes until the cod reaches an internal temperature of 64ºC on a meat thermometer and the outside is crispy. Flip the fillets halfway through the cooking time.
6. Let the fish cool for 5 minutes and serve.

Tortilla Prawn Tacos

Serves 4

Prep time: 10 minutes / Cook time: 6 minutes

Spicy Mayo:

- 3 tablespoons mayonnaise
- 1 tablespoon Louisiana-style hot pepper sauce, or Sriracha

Coriander-Lime Slaw:

- 180 g shredded green cabbage
- ½ small red onion, thinly sliced
- 1 small jalapeño, thinly sliced
- 2 tablespoons chopped fresh cilantro
- Juice of 1 lime
- ¼ teaspoon kosher salt

Prawns:

- 1 large egg, beaten
- 1 cup crushed tortilla chips
- 24 jumbo prawns (about 455 g), peeled and deveined
- ⅛ teaspoon kosher or coarse sea salt
- Cooking spray
- 8 corn tortillas, for serving

Instructions:

1. For the spicy mayo: In a small bowl, mix the mayonnaise and hot pepper sauce.
2. For the coriander-lime slaw: In a large bowl, toss together the cabbage, onion, jalapeño, coriander, lime juice, and salt to combine. Cover and refrigerate to chill.
3. For the prawns: Place the egg in a shallow bowl and the crushed tortilla chips in another. Season the prawns with the salt. Dip the prawns in the egg, then in the crumbs, pressing gently to adhere. Place on a work surface and spray both sides with oil.
4. Preheat the air fryer to 182°C.
5. Working in batches, arrange a single layer of the prawns in the air fryer basket. Air fry for 6 minutes, flipping halfway, until golden and cooked through in the center.

6. To serve, place 2 tortillas on each plate and top each with 3 prawns. Top each taco with ¼ of the slaw, then drizzle with spicy mayo.

Balsamic Tilapia

Serves 4

Prep time: 5 minutes / Cook time: 15 minutes

Ingredients:

- 4 tilapia fillets, boneless
- 2 tablespoons balsamic vinegar
- 1 teaspoon avocado oil
- 1 teaspoon dried basil

Instructions:

1. Sprinkle the tilapia fillets with balsamic vinegar, avocado oil, and dried basil.
2. Then put the fillets in the air fryer basket and cook at 185°C for 15 minutes.

Sea Bass with Potato Scales

Serves 2

Prep time: 10 minutes / Cook time: 10 minutes

Ingredients:

- 2 fillets of sea bass, 170- to 230 g each
- Salt and freshly ground black pepper, to taste
- 60 ml mayonnaise
- 2 teaspoons finely chopped lemon zest
- 1 teaspoon chopped fresh thyme
- 2 Fingerling, or new potatoes, very thinly sliced into rounds
- Olive oil
- ½ clove garlic, crushed into a paste
- 1 tablespoon capers, drained and rinsed
- 1 tablespoon olive oil
- 1 teaspoon lemon juice, to taste

Instructions:

1. Preheat the air fryer to 204°C.

2. Season the fish well with salt and freshly ground black pepper. Mix the mayonnaise, lemon zest and thyme together in a small bowl. Spread a thin layer of the mayonnaise mixture on both fillets. Start layering rows of potato slices onto the fish fillets to simulate the fish scales. The second row should overlap the first row slightly. Dabbing a little more mayonnaise along the upper edge of the row of potatoes where the next row overlaps will help the potato slices stick. Press the potatoes onto the fish to secure them well and season again with salt. Brush or spray the potato layer with olive oil.

3. Transfer the fish to the air fryer and air fry for 8 to 10 minutes, depending on the thickness of your fillets. 1-inch of fish should take 10 minutes at 204°C.

4. While the fish is cooking, add the garlic, capers, olive oil and lemon juice to the remaining mayonnaise mixture to make the caper aïoli.

5. Serve the fish warm with a dollop of the aïoli on top or on the side.

Cod with Avocado

Serves 2

Prep time: 30 minutes / Cook time: 10 minutes

Ingredients:

- 90 g shredded cabbage
- 60 ml full-fat sour cream
- 2 tablespoons full-fat mayonnaise
- 20 g chopped pickled jalapeños
- 2 (85 g) cod fillets
- 1 teaspoon chilli powder
- 1 teaspoon cumin
- ½ teaspoon paprika
- ¼ teaspoon garlic powder
- 1 medium avocado, peeled, pitted, and sliced
- ½ medium lime

Instructions:

1. In a large bowl, place cabbage, sour cream, mayonnaise, and jalapeños. Mix until fully coated. Let sit for 20 minutes in the refrigerator.

2. Sprinkle cod fillets with chilli powder, cumin, paprika, and garlic powder. Place each fillet into the air fryer basket.

3. Adjust the temperature to 188°C and set the timer for 10 minutes.

4. Flip the fillets halfway through the cooking time. When fully cooked, fish should have an internal temperature of at least 64°C.

5. To serve, divide slaw mixture into two serving bowls, break cod fillets into pieces and spread over the bowls, and top with avocado. Squeeze lime juice over each bowl. Serve immediately.

Southern-Style Catfish

Serves 4

Prep time: 10 minutes / Cook time: 12 minutes

Ingredients:

- 4 (200 g) catfish fillets
- 80 ml heavy whipping cream
- 1 tablespoon lemon juice
- 110 g blanched finely ground almond flour
- 2 teaspoons Old Bay seasoning
- ½ teaspoon salt
- ¼ teaspoon ground black pepper

Instructions:

1. Place catfish fillets into a large bowl with cream and pour in lemon juice. Stir to coat.

2. In a separate large bowl, mix flour and Old Bay seasoning.

3. Remove each fillet and gently shake off excess cream. Sprinkle with salt and pepper. Press each fillet gently into flour mixture on both sides to coat.

4. Place fillets into ungreased air fryer basket. Adjust the temperature to 204°C and air fry for 12 minutes, turning fillets halfway through cooking. Catfish will be golden brown and have an internal temperature of at least 64°C when done. Serve warm.

Panko Catfish Nuggets

Serves 4

Prep time: 10 minutes / Cook time: 7 to 8 minutes

Ingredients:

- 2 medium catfish fillets, cut into chunks (approximately 1 × 2 inch)
- Salt and pepper, to taste
- 2 eggs
- 2 tablespoons skimmed milk
- 60 g cornflour
- 150 g panko bread crumbs
- Cooking spray

Instructions:

1. Preheat the air fryer to 200°C.
2. In a medium bowl, season the fish chunks with salt and pepper to taste.
3. In a small bowl, beat together the eggs with milk until well combined.
4. Place the cornflour and bread crumbs into separate shallow dishes.
5. Dredge the fish chunks one at a time in the cornflour, coating well on both sides, then dip in the egg mixture, shaking off any excess, finally press well into the bread crumbs. Spritz the fish chunks with cooking spray.
6. Arrange the fish chunks in the air fryer basket in a single layer. You may need to cook in batches depending on the size of your air fryer basket.
7. Fry the fish chunks for 7 to 8 minutes until they are no longer translucent in the center

and golden brown. Shake the basket once during cooking.
8. Remove the fish chunks from the basket to a plate. Repeat with the remaining fish chunks.
9. Serve warm.

Prawns Curry

Serves 4

Prep time: 30 minutes / Cook time: 10 minutes

Ingredients:

- 180 ml unsweetened full-fat coconut milk
- 10 g finely chopped yellow onion
- 2 teaspoons garam masala
- 1 tablespoon minced fresh ginger
- 1 tablespoon minced garlic
- 1 teaspoon ground turmeric
- 1 teaspoon salt
- ¼ to ½ teaspoon cayenne pepper
- 455 g raw prawns (21 to 25 count), peeled and deveined
- 2 teaspoons chopped fresh coriander

Instructions:

1. In a large bowl, stir together the coconut milk, onion, garam masala, ginger, garlic, turmeric, salt and cayenne, until well blended.
2. Add the prawns and toss until coated with sauce on all sides. Marinate at room temperature for 30 minutes.
3. Transfer the prawns and marinade to a baking pan. Place the pan in the air fryer basket. Set the air fryer to 192°C for 10 minutes, stirring halfway through the cooking time.
4. Transfer the prawns to a serving bowl or platter. Sprinkle with the cilantro and serve.

Apple Cider Mussels

Serves 5

Prep time: 10 minutes / Cook time: 2 minutes

Ingredients:

- 900 g mussels, cleaned and de-bearded
- 1 teaspoon onion powder
- 1 teaspoon ground cumin
- 1 tablespoon avocado oil
- 60 ml apple cider vinegar

Instructions:

1. Mix mussels with onion powder, ground cumin, avocado oil, and apple cider vinegar.
2. Put the mussels in the air fryer and cook at 202°C for 2 minutes.

Smoky Prawns and Chorizo Tapas

Serves 2 to 4

Prep time: 15 minutes / Cook time: 10 minutes

Ingredients:

- 110 g Spanish (cured) chorizo, halved horizontally and sliced crosswise
- 230 g raw medium prawns, peeled and deveined
- 1 tablespoon extra-virgin olive oil
- 1 small shallot, halved and thinly sliced
- 1 garlic clove, minced
- 1 tablespoon finely chopped fresh oregano
- ½ teaspoon smoked Spanish paprika
- ¼ teaspoon kosher or coarse sea salt
- ¼ teaspoon black pepper
- 3 tablespoons fresh orange juice
- 1 tablespoon minced fresh parsley

Instructions:

1. Place the chorizo in a baking pan. Set the pan in the air fryer basket. Set the air fryer to 192°C for 5 minutes, or until the chorizo has started to brown and render its fat.
2. Meanwhile, in a large bowl, combine the prawns, olive oil, shallot, garlic, oregano, paprika, salt, and pepper. Toss until the prawns are well coated.
3. Transfer the prawns to the pan with the chorizo. Stir to combine. Place the pan in the air fryer basket. Cook for 10 minutes, stirring halfway through the cooking time.
4. Transfer the prawns and chorizo to a serving dish. Drizzle with the orange juice and toss to combine. Sprinkle with the parsley.

Cod with Creamy Mustard Sauce

Serves 4

Prep time: 10 minutes / Cook time: 10 minutes

Ingredients:

Fish:
- Olive or vegetable oil, for spraying
- 455 g cod fillets
- 2 tablespoons olive oil
- 1 tablespoon lemon juice
- 1 teaspoon salt
- ½ teaspoon freshly ground black pepper

Mustard Sauce:
- 120 ml heavy cream
- 3 tablespoons Dijon mustard
- 1 tablespoon unsalted butter
- 1 teaspoon salt

Instructions:

1. Make the Fish: 1. Line the air fryer basket with baking paper and spray lightly with oil.
2. Rub the cod with the olive oil and lemon juice. Season with the salt and black pepper.
3. Place the cod in the prepared basket. You may need to work in batches, depending on

the size of your air fryer.

4. Roast at 176°C for 5 minutes. Increase the temperature to 204°C and cook for another 5 minutes, until flaky and the internal temperature reaches 64°C. Make the Mustard Sauce: 5. In a small saucepan, mix together the heavy cream, mustard, butter, and salt and bring to a simmer over low heat. Cook for 3 to 4 minutes, or until the sauce starts to thicken.

6. Transfer the cod to a serving plate and drizzle with the mustard sauce. Serve immediately.

Tuna Patties with Spicy Sriracha Sauce

Serves 4

Prep time: 10 minutes / Cook time: 10 minutes

Ingredients:

- 2 (170 g) cans tuna packed in oil, drained
- 3 tablespoons almond flour
- 2 tablespoons mayonnaise
- 1 teaspoon dried dill
- ½ teaspoon onion powder
- Pinch of salt and pepper
- Spicy Sriracha Sauce:
- 60 g mayonnaise
- 1 tablespoon Sriracha sauce
- 1 teaspoon garlic powder

Instructions:

1. Preheat the air fryer to 192°C. Line the basket with baking paper.

2. In a large bowl, combine the tuna, almond flour, mayonnaise, dill, and onion powder. Season to taste with salt and freshly ground black pepper. Use a fork to stir, mashing with the back of the fork as necessary, until thoroughly combined.

3. Use an ice cream scoop to form the tuna mixture patties. Place the patties in a single layer on the baking paper in the air fryer basket. Press lightly with the bottom of the scoop to flatten into a circle about ½ inch thick. Pausing halfway through the cooking time to turn the patties, air fry for 10 minutes until lightly browned.

4. To make the Sriracha sauce: In a small bowl, combine the mayonnaise, Sriracha, and garlic powder. Serve the tuna patties topped with the Sriracha sauce.

CHAPTER 4 POULTRY RECIPES

Herb-Buttermilk Chicken Breast

Serves 2

Prep time: 5 minutes / Cook time: 40 minutes

Ingredients:

- 1 large bone-in, skin-on chicken breast
- 240 ml buttermilk
- 1½ teaspoons dried parsley
- 1½ teaspoons dried chives
- ¾ teaspoon kosher salt
- ½ teaspoon dried dill
- ½ teaspoon onion powder
- ¼ teaspoon garlic powder
- ¼ teaspoon dried tarragon
- Cooking spray

Instructions:

1. Place the chicken breast in a bowl and pour over the buttermilk, turning the chicken in it to make sure it's completely covered. Let the chicken stand at room temperature for at least 20 minutes or in the refrigerator for up to 4 hours.
2. Meanwhile, in a bowl, stir together the parsley, chives, salt, dill, onion powder, garlic powder, and tarragon.
3. Preheat the air fryer to 150°C.
4. Remove the chicken from the buttermilk, letting the excess drip off, then place the chicken skin-side up directly in the air fryer. Sprinkle the seasoning mix all over the top of the chicken breast, then let stand until the herb mix soaks into the buttermilk, at least 5 minutes.
5. Spray the top of the chicken with cooking spray. Bake for 10 minutes, then increase the temperature to 180°C and bake until an instant-read thermometer inserted into the thickest part of the breast reads 80°C and the chicken is deep golden brown, 30 to 35 minutes.
6. Transfer the chicken breast to a cutting board, let rest for 10 minutes, then cut the meat off the bone and cut into thick slices for serving.

Crispy Dill Chicken Strips

Serves 4

Prep time: 30 minutes / Cook time: 10 minutes

Ingredients:

- 2 whole boneless, skinless chicken breasts (about 450 g each), halved lengthwise
- 230 ml Italian dressing
- 110 g finely crushed crisps
- 1 tablespoon dried dill weed
- 1 tablespoon garlic powder
- 1 large egg, beaten
- 1 to 2 tablespoons oil

Instructions:

1. In a large resealable bag, combine the chicken and Italian dressing. Seal the bag and refrigerate to marinate at least 1 hour.
2. In a shallow dish, stir together the potato chips, dill, and garlic powder. Place the beaten egg in a second shallow dish.
3. Remove the chicken from the marinade. Roll the chicken pieces in the egg and the crisp mixture, coating thoroughly.
4. Preheat the air fryer to 170°C. Line the air fryer basket with parchment paper.
5. Place the coated chicken on the parchment and spritz with oil.
6. Cook for 5 minutes. Flip the chicken, spritz

it with oil, and cook for 5 minutes more until the outsides are crispy and the insides are no longer pink.

Wild Rice and Kale Stuffed Chicken Thighs

Serves 4

Prep time: 10 minutes / Cook time: 22 minutes

Ingredients:

- 4 boneless, skinless chicken thighs
- 250 g cooked wild rice
- 35 g chopped kale
- 2 garlic cloves, minced
- 1 teaspoon salt
- Juice of 1 lemon
- 100 g crumbled feta
- Olive oil cooking spray
- 1 tablespoon olive oi

Instructions:

1. Preheat the air fryer to 192ºC.
2. Place the chicken thighs between two pieces of plastic wrap, and using a meat mallet or a rolling pin, pound them out to about ¼-inch thick.
3. In a medium bowl, combine the rice, kale, garlic, salt, and lemon juice and mix well.
4. Place a quarter of the rice mixture into the middle of each chicken thigh, then sprinkle 2 tablespoons of feta over the filling.
5. Spray the air fryer basket with olive oil cooking spray.
6. Fold the sides of the chicken thigh over the filling, and then gently place each of them seam-side down into the air fryer basket. Brush each stuffed chicken thigh with olive oil.
7. Roast the stuffed chicken thighs for 12 minutes, then turn them over and cook for an additional 10 minutes, or until the internal temperature reaches 76ºC.

Chicken Hand Pies

Makes 8 pies

Prep time: 30 minutes / Cook time: 10 minutes per batch

Ingredients:

- 180 ml chicken broth
- 130 g frozen mixed peas and carrots
- 140 g cooked chicken, chopped
- 1 tablespoon cornflour
- 1 tablespoon milk
- Salt and pepper, to taste
- 1 (8-count) can organic flaky biscuits
- Oil for misting or cooking spray

Instructions:

1. In a medium saucepan, bring chicken broth to a boil. Stir in the frozen peas and carrots and cook for 5 minutes over medium heat. Stir in chicken.
2. Mix the cornflour into the milk until it dissolves. Stir it into the simmering chicken broth mixture and cook just until thickened.
3. Remove from heat, add salt and pepper to taste, and let cool slightly.
4. Lay biscuits out on wax paper. Peel each biscuit apart in the middle to make 2 rounds so you have 16 rounds total. Using your hands or a rolling pin, flatten each biscuit round slightly to make it larger and thinner.
5. Divide chicken filling among 8 of the biscuit rounds. Place remaining biscuit rounds on top and press edges all around. Use the tines of a fork to crimp biscuit edges and make sure they are sealed well.
6. Spray both sides lightly with oil or cooking spray.
7. Cook in a single layer, 4 at a time, at 170ºC for 10 minutes or until biscuit dough is cooked through and golden brown.

Stuffed Chicken Florentine

Serves 4

Prep time: 10 minutes / Cook time: 20 minutes

Ingredients:

- 3 tablespoons pine nuts
- 40 g frozen spinach, thawed and squeezed dry
- 75 g ricotta cheese
- 2 tablespoons grated Parmesan cheese
- 3 cloves garlic, minced
- Salt and freshly ground black pepper, to taste
- 4 small boneless, skinless chicken breast halves (about 680 g)
- 8 slices bacon

Instructions:

1. Place the pine nuts in a small pan and set in the air fryer basket. Set the air fryer to 200°C and air fry for 2 to 3 minutes until toasted. Remove the pine nuts to a mixing bowl and continue preheating the air fryer.
2. In a large bowl, combine the spinach, ricotta, Parmesan, and garlic. Season to taste with salt and pepper and stir well until thoroughly combined.
3. Using a sharp knife, cut into the chicken breasts, slicing them across and opening them up like a book, but be careful not to cut them all the way through. Sprinkle the chicken with salt and pepper.
4. Spoon equal amounts of the spinach mixture into the chicken, then fold the top of the chicken breast back over the top of the stuffing. Wrap each chicken breast with 2 slices of bacon.
5. Working in batches if necessary, air fry the chicken for 18 to 20 minutes until the bacon is crisp and a thermometer inserted into the thickest part of the chicken registers 76°C.

Classic Whole Chicken

Serves 4

Prep time: 5 minutes / Cook time: 50 minutes

Ingredients:

- Oil, for spraying
- 1 (1. 8 kg) whole chicken, giblets removed
- 1 tablespoon olive oil
- 1 teaspoon paprika
- ½ teaspoon granulated garlic
- ½ teaspoon salt
- ½ teaspoon freshly ground black pepper
- ¼ teaspoon finely chopped fresh parsley, for garnish

Instructions:

1. Line the air fryer basket with parchment and spray lightly with oil.
2. Pat the chicken dry with paper towels. Rub it with the olive oil until evenly coated.
3. In a small bowl, mix together the paprika, garlic, salt, and black pepper and sprinkle it evenly over the chicken.
4. Place the chicken in the prepared basket, breast-side down.
5. Air fry at 180°C for 30 minutes, flip, and cook for another 20 minutes, or until the internal temperature reaches 76°C and the juices run clear.
6. Sprinkle with the parsley before serving.

Peanut Butter Chicken Satay

Serves 4

Prep time: 12 minutes / Cook time: 12 to 18 minutes

Ingredients:

- 120 g crunchy peanut butter
- 80 ml chicken broth
- 3 tablespoons low-sodium soy sauce
- 2 tablespoons freshly squeezed lemon juice

- 2 garlic cloves, minced
- 2 tablespoons extra-virgin olive oil
- 1 teaspoon curry powder
- 450 g chicken tenders
- Cooking oil spray

Instructions:

1. In a medium bowl, whisk the peanut butter, broth, soy sauce, lemon juice, garlic, olive oil, and curry powder until smooth.
2. Place 2 tablespoons of this mixture into a small bowl. Transfer the remaining sauce to a serving bowl and set aside.
3. Add the chicken tenders to the bowl with the 2 tablespoons of sauce and stir to coat. Let stand for a few minutes to marinate.
4. Insert the crisper plate into the basket and the basket into the unit. Preheat the unit by selecting AIR FRY, setting the temperature to 200°C, and setting the time to 3 minutes. Select START/STOP to begin.
5. Run a 6-inch bamboo skewer lengthwise through each chicken tender.
6. Once the unit is preheated, spray the crisper plate with cooking oil. Working in batches, place half the chicken skewers into the basket in a single layer without overlapping.
7. Select AIR FRY, set the temperature to 200°C, and set the time to 9 minutes. Select START/STOP to begin.
8. After 6 minutes, check the chicken. If a food thermometer inserted into the chicken registers 76°C, it is done. If not, resume cooking.
9. Repeat steps 6, 7, and 8 with the remaining chicken.
10. When the cooking is complete, serve the chicken with the reserved sauce.

Spice-Rubbed Turkey Breast

Serves 10

Prep time: 5 minutes / Cook time: 45 to 55 minutes

Ingredients:

- 1 tablespoon sea salt
- 1 teaspoon paprika
- 1 teaspoon onion powder
- 1 teaspoon garlic powder
- ½ teaspoon freshly ground black
- 1.8 kg bone-in, skin-on turkey breast
- 2 tablespoons unsalted butter, melted

Instructions:

1. In a small bowl, combine the salt, paprika, onion powder, garlic powder, and pepper.
2. Sprinkle the seasonings all over the turkey. Brush the turkey with some of the melted butter.
3. Set the air fryer to 180°C. . Place the turkey in the air fryer basket, skin-side down, and roast for 25 minutes.
4. Flip the turkey and brush it with the remaining butter. Continue cooking for another 20 to 30 minutes, until an instant-read thermometer reads 70°C.
5. Remove the turkey breast from the air fryer. Tent a piece of aluminum foil over the turkey, and allow it to rest for about 5 minutes before serving.

Chicken Nuggets

Serves 4

Prep time: 10 minutes / Cook time: 15 minutes

Ingredients:

- 450 g chicken mince thighs
- 110 g shredded Mozzarella cheese
- 1 large egg, whisked
- ½ teaspoon salt
- ¼ teaspoon dried oregano
- ¼ teaspoon garlic powder

Instructions:

1. In a large bowl, combine all ingredients.

Form mixture into twenty nugget shapes, about 2 tablespoons each.

2. Place nuggets into ungreased air fryer basket, working in batches if needed. Adjust the temperature to (190°C and air fry for 15 minutes, turning nuggets halfway through cooking. Let cool 5 minutes before serving.

Greek Chicken Souvlaki

Serves 3 to 4

Prep time: 30 minutes / Cook time: 15 minutes

Ingredients:

Chicken:
- Grated zest and juice of 1 lemon
- 2 tablespoons extra-virgin olive oil
- 1 tablespoon Greek souvlaki seasoning
- 450 g boneless, skinless chicken breast, cut into 2-inch chunks
- Vegetable oil spray

For Serving:
- Warm pita bread or hot cooked rice
- Sliced ripe tomatoes
- Sliced cucumbers
- Thinly sliced red onion
- Kalamata olives
- Tzatziki

Instructions:

1. For the chicken: In a small bowl, combine the lemon zest, lemon juice, olive oil, and souvlaki seasoning. Place the chicken in a gallon-size resealable plastic bag. Pour the marinade over chicken. Seal bag and massage to coat. Place the bag in a large bowl and marinate for 30 minutes, or cover and refrigerate up to 24 hours, turning the bag occasionally.
2. Place the chicken a single layer in the air fryer basket. Set the air fryer to 180°C for 10 minutes, turning the chicken and spraying

with a little vegetable oil spray halfway through the cooking time. Increase the air fryer temperature to 200°C for 5 minutes to allow the chicken to crisp and brown a little.

3. Transfer the chicken to a serving platter and serve with pita bread or rice, tomatoes, cucumbers, onion, olives and tzatziki.

Chicken Paillard

Serves 2

Prep time: 10 minutes / Cook time: 10 minutes

Ingredients:

- 2 large eggs, room temperature
- 1 tablespoon water
- 40 g powdered Parmesan cheese or pork dust
- 2 teaspoons dried thyme leaves
- 1 teaspoon ground black pepper
- 2 (140 g) boneless, skinless chicken breasts, pounded to ½ inch thick
- Lemon Butter Sauce:
- 2 tablespoons unsalted butter, melted
- 2 teaspoons lemon juice
- ¼ teaspoon finely chopped fresh thyme leaves, plus more for garnish
- ⅛ teaspoon fine sea salt
- Lemon slices, for serving

Instructions:

1. Spray the air fryer basket with avocado oil. Preheat the air fryer to 200°C.
2. Beat the eggs in a shallow dish, then add the water and stir well.
3. In a separate shallow dish, mix together the Parmesan, thyme, and pepper until well combined.
4. One at a time, dip the chicken breasts in the eggs and let any excess drip off, then dredge both sides of the chicken in the Parmesan mixture. As you finish, set the coated chicken in the air fryer basket.

5. Roast the chicken in the air fryer for 5 minutes, then flip the chicken and cook for another 5 minutes, or until cooked through and the internal temperature reaches 76°C.

6. While the chicken cooks, make the lemon butter sauce: In a small bowl, mix together all the sauce ingredients until well combined.

7. Plate the chicken and pour the sauce over it. Garnish with chopped fresh thyme and serve with lemon slices.

8. Store leftovers in an airtight container in the refrigerator for up to 4 days. Reheat in a preheated 200°C air fryer for 5 minutes, or until heated through.

Barbecue Chicken Bites

Serves 4

Prep time: 5 minutes / Cook time: 19 minutes

Ingredients:

- Oil, for spraying
- 2 (170 g) boneless, skinless chicken breasts, cut into bite-size pieces
- 60 g all-purpose flour
- 1 tablespoon granulated garlic
- 2 teaspoons seasoned salt
- 280 g barbecue sauce

Instructions:

1. Line the air fryer basket with parchment and spray lightly with oil.
2. Place the chicken, flour, garlic, and seasoned salt in a zip-top plastic bag, seal, and shake well until evenly coated.
3. Place the chicken in an even layer in the prepared basket and spray liberally with oil. You may need to work in batches, depending on the size of your air fryer.
4. Roast at 200°C for 8 minutes, flip, spray with more oil, and cook for another 8 minutes, or until the internal temperature reaches 76°C

and the juices run clear.

5. Transfer the chicken to a large bowl and toss with the barbecue sauce.

6. Line the air fryer basket with fresh parchment, return the chicken to the basket, and cook for another 3 minutes.

Chicken with Lettuce

Serves 4

Prep time: 15 minutes / Cook time: 14 minutes

Ingredients:

- 450 g chicken breast tenders, chopped into bite-size pieces
- ½ onion, thinly sliced
- ½ red bell pepper, seeded and thinly sliced
- ½ green bell pepper, seeded and thinly sliced
- 1 tablespoon olive oil
- 1 tablespoon fajita seasoning
- 1 teaspoon kosher salt
- Juice of ½ lime
- 8 large lettuce leaves
- 230 g prepared guacamole

Instructions:

1. Preheat the air fryer to 200°C.
2. In a large bowl, combine the chicken, onion, and peppers. Drizzle with the olive oil and toss until thoroughly coated. Add the fajita seasoning and salt and toss again.
3. Working in batches if necessary, arrange the chicken and vegetables in a single layer in the air fryer basket. Pausing halfway through the cooking time to shake the basket, air fry for 14 minutes, or until the vegetables are tender and a thermometer inserted into the thickest piece of chicken registers 76°C.
4. Transfer the mixture to a serving platter and drizzle with the fresh lime juice. Serve with the lettuce leaves and top with the guacamole.

Cranberry Curry Chicken

Serves 4

Prep time: 12 minutes / Cook time: 18 minutes

Ingredients:

- 3 (140 g) low-sodium boneless, skinless chicken breasts, cut into 1½-inch cubes
- 2 teaspoons olive oil
- 2 tablespoons cornflour
- 1 tablespoon curry powder
- 1 tart apple, chopped
- 120 ml low-sodium chicken broth
- 60 g dried cranberries
- 2 tablespoons freshly squeezed orange juice
- Brown rice, cooked (optional)

Instructions:

1. Preheat the air fryer to 196ºC.
2. In a medium bowl, mix the chicken and olive oil. Sprinkle with the cornflour and curry powder. Toss to coat. Stir in the apple and transfer to a metal pan. Bake in the air fryer for 8 minutes, stirring once during cooking.
3. Add the chicken broth, cranberries, and orange juice. Bake for about 10 minutes more, or until the sauce is slightly thickened and the chicken reaches an internal temperature of 76ºC on a meat thermometer. Serve over hot cooked brown rice, if desired.

Almond-Crusted Chicken

Serves 4

Prep time: 15 minutes / Cook time: 25 minutes

Ingredients:

- 20 g slivered almonds
- 2 (170 g) boneless, skinless chicken breasts
- 2 tablespoons full-fat mayonnaise
- 1 tablespoon Dijon mustard

Instructions:

1. Pulse the almonds in a food processor or chop until finely chopped. Place almonds evenly on a plate and set aside.
2. Completely slice each chicken breast in half lengthwise.
3. Mix the mayonnaise and mustard in a small bowl and then coat chicken with the mixture.
4. Lay each piece of chicken in the chopped almonds to fully coat. Carefully move the pieces into the air fryer basket.
5. Adjust the temperature to 180ºC and air fry for 25 minutes.
6. Chicken will be done when it has reached an internal temperature of 76ºC or more. Serve warm.

African Piri-Piri Chicken Drumsticks

Serves 2

Prep time: 30 minutes / Cook time: 20 minutes

Ingredients:

- Chicken:
- 1 tablespoon chopped fresh thyme leaves
- 1 tablespoon minced fresh ginger
- 1 small shallot, finely chopped
- 2 garlic cloves, minced
- 80 ml piri-piri sauce or hot sauce
- 3 tablespoons extra-virgin olive oil
- Zest and juice of 1 lemon
- 1 teaspoon smoked paprika
- ½ teaspoon kosher salt
- ½ teaspoon black pepper
- 4 chicken drumsticks
- Glaze:
- 2 tablespoons butter or ghee
- 1 teaspoon chopped fresh thyme leaves
- 1 garlic clove, minced
- 1 tablespoon piri-piri sauce

- 1 tablespoon fresh lemon juice

Instructions:

1. For the chicken: In a small bowl, stir together all the ingredients except the chicken. Place the chicken and the marinade in a gallon-size resealable plastic bag. Seal the bag and massage to coat. Refrigerate for at least 2 hours or up to 24 hours, turning the bag occasionally.
2. Place the chicken legs in the air fryer basket. Set the air fryer to 200°C for 20 minutes, turning the chicken halfway through the cooking time.
3. Meanwhile, for the glaze: Melt the butter in a small saucepan over medium-high heat. Add the thyme and garlic. Cook, stirring, until the garlic just begins to brown, 1 to 2 minutes. Add the piri-piri sauce and lemon juice. Reduce the heat to medium-low and simmer for 1 to 2 minutes.
4. Transfer the chicken to a serving platter. Pour the glaze over the chicken. Serve immediately.

Lemon Chicken with Garlic

Serves 4

Prep time: 5 minutes / Cook time: 20 to 25 minutes

Ingredients:

- 8 bone-in chicken thighs, skin on
- 1 tablespoon olive oil
- 1½ teaspoons lemon-pepper seasoning
- ½ teaspoon paprika
- ½ teaspoon garlic powder
- ¼ teaspoon freshly ground black pepper
- Juice of ½ lemon

Instructions:

1. Preheat the air fryer to 180°C.
2. Place the chicken in a large bowl and drizzle

with the olive oil. Top with the lemon-pepper seasoning, paprika, garlic powder, and freshly ground black pepper. Toss until thoroughly coated.
3. Working in batches if necessary, arrange the chicken in a single layer in the basket of the air fryer. Pausing halfway through the cooking time to turn the chicken, air fry for 20 to 25 minutes, until a thermometer inserted into the thickest piece registers 76°C.
4. Transfer the chicken to a serving platter and squeeze the lemon juice over the top.

Turkish Chicken Kebabs

Serves 4

Prep time: 30 minutes / Cook time: 15 minutes

Ingredients:

- 70 g plain Greek yogurt
- 1 tablespoon minced garlic
- 1 tablespoon tomato paste
- 1 tablespoon fresh lemon juice
- 1 tablespoon vegetable oil
- 1 teaspoon kosher salt
- 1 teaspoon ground cumin
- 1 teaspoon sweet Hungarian paprika
- ½ teaspoon ground cinnamon
- ½ teaspoon black pepper
- ½ teaspoon cayenne pepper
- 450 g boneless, skinless chicken thighs, quartered crosswise

Instructions:

1. In a large bowl, combine the yogurt, garlic, tomato paste, lemon juice, vegetable oil, salt, cumin, paprika, cinnamon, black pepper, and cayenne. Stir until the spices are blended into the yogurt.
2. Add the chicken to the bowl and toss until well coated. Marinate at room temperature

for 30 minutes, or cover and refrigerate for up to 24 hours.

3. Arrange the chicken in a single layer in the air fryer basket. Set the air fryer to (190ºC for 10 minutes. Turn the chicken and cook for 5 minutes more. Use a meat thermometer to ensure the chicken has reached an internal temperature of 76ºC.

Herbed Roast Chicken Breast

Serves 2 to 4

Prep time: 10 minutes / Cook time: 25 minutes

Ingredients:

- 2 tablespoons salted butter or ghee, at room temperature
- 1 teaspoon dried Italian seasoning, crushed
- ½ teaspoon kosher salt
- ½ teaspoon smoked paprika
- ¼ teaspoon black pepper
- 2 bone-in, skin-on chicken breast halves (280 g each)
- Lemon wedges, for serving

Instructions:

1. In a small bowl, stir together the butter, Italian seasoning, salt, paprika, and pepper until thoroughly combined.
2. Using a small sharp knife, carefully loosen the skin on each chicken breast half, starting at the thin end of each. Very carefully separate the skin from the flesh, leaving the skin attached at the thick end of each breast. Divide the herb butter into quarters. Rub one-quarter of the butter onto the flesh of each breast. Fold and lightly press the skin back onto each breast. Rub the remaining butter onto the skin of each breast.
3. Place the chicken in the air fryer basket. Set the air fryer to (190ºC for 25 minutes. Use a meat thermometer to ensure the chicken

breasts have reached an internal temperature of 76ºC.

4. Transfer the chicken to a cutting board. Lightly cover with aluminum foil and let rest for 5 to 10 minutes.
5. Serve with lemon wedges.

Fiesta Chicken Plate

Serves 4

Prep time: 15 minutes / Cook time: 12 to 15 minutes

Ingredients:

- 450 g boneless, skinless chicken breasts (2 large breasts)
- 2 tablespoons lime juice
- 1 teaspoon cumin
- ½ teaspoon salt
- 40 g grated Pepper Jack cheese
- 1 (455 g) can refried beans
- 130 g salsa
- 30 g shredded lettuce
- 1 medium tomato, chopped
- 2 avocados, peeled and sliced
- 1 small onion, sliced into thin rings
- Sour cream
- Tortilla chips (optional)

Instructions:

1. Split each chicken breast in half lengthwise.
2. Mix lime juice, cumin, and salt together and brush on all surfaces of chicken breasts.
3. Place in air fryer basket and air fry at 200ºC for 12 to 15 minutes, until well done.
4. Divide the cheese evenly over chicken breasts and cook for an additional minute to melt cheese.
5. While chicken is cooking, heat refried beans on stovetop or in microwave.
6. When ready to serve, divide beans among 4 plates. Place chicken breasts on top of beans and spoon salsa over. Arrange the lettuce,

tomatoes, and avocados artfully on each plate and scatter with the onion rings.

7. Pass sour cream at the table and serve with tortilla chips if desired.

Juicy Paprika Chicken Breast

Serves 4

Prep time: 5 minutes / Cook time: 30 minutes

Ingredients:

- Oil, for spraying
- 4 (170 g) boneless, skinless chicken breasts
- 1 tablespoon olive oil
- 1 tablespoon paprika
- 1 tablespoon packed light brown sugar
- ½ teaspoon cayenne pepper
- ½ teaspoon onion powder
- ½ teaspoon granulated garlic

Instructions:

1. Line the air fryer basket with parchment and spray lightly with oil.
2. Brush the chicken with the olive oil.
3. In a small bowl, mix together the paprika, brown sugar, cayenne pepper, onion powder, and garlic and sprinkle it over the chicken.
4. Place the chicken in the prepared basket. You may need to work in batches, depending on the size of your air fryer.
5. Air fry at 180°C for 15 minutes, flip, and cook for another 15 minutes, or until the internal temperature reaches 76°C. Serve immediately.

Yellow Curry Chicken Thighs with Peanuts

Serves 6

Prep time: 10 minutes / Cook time: 20 minutes

Ingredients:

- 120 ml unsweetened full-fat coconut milk
- 2 tablespoons yellow curry paste
- 1 tablespoon minced fresh ginger
- 1 tablespoon minced garlic
- 1 teaspoon kosher salt
- 450 g boneless, skinless chicken thighs, halved crosswise
- 2 tablespoons chopped peanuts

Instructions:

1. In a large bowl, stir together the coconut milk, curry paste, ginger, garlic, and salt until well blended. Add the chicken; toss well to coat. Marinate at room temperature for 30 minutes, or cover and refrigerate for up to 24 hours.
2. Preheat the air fryer to 190°C.
3. Place the chicken (along with marinade) in a baking pan. Place the pan in the air fryer basket. Bake for 20 minutes, turning the chicken halfway through the cooking time. Use a meat thermometer to ensure the chicken has reached an internal temperature of 76°C.
4. Sprinkle the chicken with the chopped peanuts and serve.

Chipotle Aioli Wings

Serves 6

Prep time: 5 minutes / Cook time: 25 minutes

Ingredients:

- 900 g bone-in chicken wings
- ½ teaspoon salt
- ¼ teaspoon ground black pepper
- 2 tablespoons mayonnaise
- 2 teaspoons chipotle powder
- 2 tablespoons lemon juice

Instructions:

1. In a large bowl, toss wings in salt and pepper, then place into ungreased air fryer basket. Adjust the temperature to 200°C and air fry for 25 minutes, shaking the basket twice while cooking. Wings will be done when golden and have an internal temperature of at least 76°C.
2. In a small bowl, whisk together mayonnaise, chipotle powder, and lemon juice. Place cooked wings into a large serving bowl and drizzle with aioli. Toss to coat. Serve warm.

Pecan-Crusted Chicken Tenders

Serves 4

Prep time: 10 minutes / Cook time: 12 minutes

Ingredients:

- 2 tablespoons mayonnaise
- 1 teaspoon Dijon mustard
- 455 g boneless, skinless chicken tenders
- ½ teaspoon salt
- ¼ teaspoon ground black pepper
- 75 g chopped roasted pecans, finely ground

Instructions:

1. In a small bowl, whisk mayonnaise and mustard until combined. Brush mixture onto chicken tenders on both sides, then sprinkle tenders with salt and pepper.
2. Place pecans in a medium bowl and press each tender into pecans to coat each side.
3. Place tenders into ungreased air fryer basket in a single layer, working in batches if needed. Adjust the temperature to (190°C and roast for 12 minutes, turning tenders halfway through cooking. Tenders will be golden brown and have an internal temperature of at least 76°C when done. Serve warm.

Teriyaki Chicken Legs

Serves 2

Prep time: 12 minutes / Cook time: 18 to 20 minutes

Ingredients:

- 4 tablespoons teriyaki sauce
- 1 tablespoon orange juice
- 1 teaspoon smoked paprika
- 4 chicken legs
- Cooking spray

Instructions:

1. Mix together the teriyaki sauce, orange juice, and smoked paprika. Brush on all sides of chicken legs.
2. Spray the air fryer basket with nonstick cooking spray and place chicken in basket.
3. Air fry at 180°C for 6 minutes. Turn and baste with sauce. Cook for 6 more minutes, turn and baste. Cook for 6 to 8 minutes more, until juices run clear when chicken is pierced with a fork.

CHAPTER 5 BEEF, PORK AND LAMB

Lamb and Cucumber Burgers

Serves 4

Prep time: 8 minutes / Cook time: 15 to 18 minutes

Ingredients:

- 1 teaspoon ground ginger
- ½ teaspoon ground coriander
- ¼ teaspoon freshly ground white pepper
- ½ teaspoon ground cinnamon
- ½ teaspoon dried oregano
- ¼ teaspoon ground allspice
- ¼ teaspoon ground turmeric
- 120 ml low-fat plain Greek yogurt
- 450 g lamb mince
- 1 teaspoon garlic paste
- ¼ teaspoon salt
- ¼ teaspoon freshly ground black pepper
- Cooking oil spray
- 4 hamburger buns
- ½ cucumber, thinly sliced

Instructions:

1. In a small bowl, stir together the ginger, coriander, white pepper, cinnamon, oregano, allspice, and turmeric.
2. Put the yogurt in a small bowl and add half the spice mixture. Mix well and refrigerate.
3. Insert the crisper plate into the basket and the basket into the unit. Preheat the unit by selecting AIR FRY, setting the temperature to 182°C, and setting the time to 3 minutes. Select START/STOP to begin.
4. In a large bowl, combine the lamb, garlic paste, remaining spice mix, salt, and pepper. Gently but thoroughly mix the ingredients with your hands. Form the meat into 4 patties.
5. Once the unit is preheated, spray the crisper plate with cooking oil, and place the patties into the basket.
6. Select AIR FRY, set the temperature to 182°C, and set the time to 18 minutes. Select START/STOP to begin.
7. After 15 minutes, check the burgers. If a food thermometer inserted into the burgers registers 72°C, the burgers are done. If not, resume cooking.
8. When the cooking is complete, assemble the burgers on the buns with cucumber slices and a dollop of the yogurt dip.

Rosemary Roast Beef

Serves 8

Prep time: 30 minutes / Cook time: 30 to 35 minutes

Ingredients:

- 1 (900 g) beef roasting joint, tied with kitchen string
- Sea salt and freshly ground black pepper, to taste
- 2 teaspoons minced garlic
- 2 tablespoons finely chopped fresh rosemary
- 60 ml avocado oil

Instructions:

1. Season the roast generously with salt and pepper.
2. In a small bowl, whisk together the garlic, rosemary, and avocado oil. Rub this all over the roast. Cover loosely with aluminum foil or plastic wrap and refrigerate for at least 12 hours or up to 2 days.
3. Remove the roast from the refrigerator and allow to sit at room temperature for about 1 hour.
4. Set the air fryer to 164°C. Place the roast in

the air fryer basket and roast for 15 minutes. Flip the roast and cook for 15 to 20 minutes more, until the meat is browned and an instant-read thermometer reads 49°C at the thickest part (for medium-rare).

5. Transfer the meat to a cutting board, and let it rest for 15 minutes before thinly slicing and serving.

Pork and Pinto Bean Gorditas

Prep timePork and Pinto Bean Gorditas

Ingredients:

- 450 g lean pork mince
- 2 tablespoons chili powder
- 2 tablespoons ground cumin
- 1 teaspoon dried oregano
- 2 teaspoons paprika
- 1 teaspoon garlic powder
- 120 ml water
- 1 (425 g) can pinto beans, drained and rinsed
- 120 ml salsa
- Salt and freshly ground black pepper, to taste
- 475 ml grated Cheddar cheese
- 5 (12-inch) flour tortillas
- 4 (8-inch) crispy corn taco shells
- 1 L shredded lettuce
- 1 tomato, diced
- 80 ml sliced black olives
- Sour cream, for serving
- Tomato salsa, for serving
- Cooking spray

Instructions:

1. Preheat the air fryer to 204°C. Spritz the air fryer basket with cooking spray.
2. Put the pork in the air fryer basket and air fry at 204°C for 10 minutes, stirring a few times to gently break up the meat. Combine the chili powder, cumin, oregano, paprika, garlic powder and water in a small bowl.

Stir the spice mixture into the browned pork. Stir in the beans and salsa and air fry for an additional minute. Transfer the pork mixture to a bowl. Season with salt and freshly ground black pepper.

3. Sprinkle 120 ml of the grated cheese in the center of the flour tortillas, leaving a 2-inch border around the edge free of cheese and filling. Divide the pork mixture among the four tortillas, placing it on top of the cheese. Put a taco shell on top of the pork and top with shredded lettuce, diced tomatoes, and black olives. Cut the remaining flour tortilla into 4 quarters. These quarters of tortilla will serve as the bottom of the gordita. Put one quarter tortilla on top of each gordita and fold the edges of the bottom flour tortilla up over the sides, enclosing the filling. While holding the seams down, brush the bottom of the gordita with olive oil and place the seam side down on the countertop while you finish the remaining three gorditas.
4. Adjust the temperature to 192°C.
5. Air fry one gordita at a time. Transfer the gordita carefully to the air fryer basket, seam side down. Brush or spray the top tortilla with oil and air fry for 5 minutes. Carefully turn the gordita over and air fry for an additional 4 to 5 minutes until both sides are browned. When finished air frying all four gorditas, layer them back into the air fryer for an additional minute to make sure they are all warm before serving with sour cream and salsa.

Garlic Balsamic London Broil

Serves 8

Prep time: 30 minutes / Cook time: 8 to 10 minutes

Ingredients:

- 900 g bavette or skirt steak

- 3 large garlic cloves, minced
- 3 tablespoons balsamic vinegar
- 3 tablespoons wholegrain mustard
- 2 tablespoons olive oil
- Sea salt and ground black pepper, to taste
- ½ teaspoon dried hot red pepper flakes

Instructions:

1. Score both sides of the cleaned steak.
2. Thoroughly combine the remaining ingredients; massage this mixture into the meat to coat it on all sides. Let it marinate for at least 3 hours.
3. Set the air fryer to 204°C; Then cook the steak for 15 minutes. Flip it over and cook another 10 to 12 minutes. Bon appétit!

Italian Sausages with Peppers and Onions

Serves 3

Prep time: 5 minutes / Cook time: 28 minutes

Ingredients:

- 1 medium onion, thinly sliced
- 1 yellow or orange pepper, thinly sliced
- 1 red pepper, thinly sliced
- 60 ml avocado oil or melted coconut oil
- 1 teaspoon fine sea salt
- 6 Italian-seasoned sausages
- Dijon mustard, for serving (optional)

Instructions:

1. Preheat the air fryer to 204°C.
2. Place the onion and peppers in a large bowl. Drizzle with the oil and toss well to coat the veggies. Season with the salt.
3. Place the onion and peppers in a pie pan and cook in the air fryer for 8 minutes, stirring halfway through. Remove from the air fryer and set aside.
4. Spray the air fryer basket with avocado oil.

Place the sausages in the air fryer basket and air fry for 20 minutes, or until crispy and golden brown. During the last minute or two of cooking, add the onion and peppers to the basket with the sausages to warm them through.

5. Place the onion and peppers on a serving platter and arrange the sausages on top. Serve Dijon mustard on the side, if desired.
6. Store leftovers in an airtight container in the fridge for up to 7 days or in the freezer for up to a month. Reheat in a preheated 200°C air fryer for 3 minutes, or until heated through.

Blackened Cajun Pork Roast

Serves 4

Prep time: 20 minutes / Cook time: 33 minutes

Ingredients:

- 900 g bone-in pork loin roast
- 2 tablespoons oil
- 60 ml Cajun seasoning
- 120 ml diced onion
- 120 ml diced celery
- 120 ml diced green pepper
- 1 tablespoon minced garlic

Instructions:

1. Cut 5 slits across the pork roast. Spritz it with oil, coating it completely. Evenly sprinkle the Cajun seasoning over the pork roast.
2. In a medium bowl, stir together the onion, celery, green pepper, and garlic until combined. Set aside.
3. Preheat the air fryer to 182°C. Line the air fryer basket with parchment paper.
4. Place the pork roast on the parchment and spritz with oil.
5. Cook for 5 minutes. Flip the roast and cook for 5 minutes more. Continue to flip and

cook in 5-minute increments for a total cook time of 20 minutes.

6. Increase the air fryer temperature to 200°C.

7. Cook the roast for 8 minutes more and flip. Add the vegetable mixture to the basket and cook for a final 5 minutes. Let the roast sit for 5 minutes before serving.

Rosemary Ribeye Steaks

Serves 2

Prep time: 10 minutes / Cook time: 15 minutes

Ingredients:
- 60 ml butter
- 1 clove garlic, minced
- Salt and ground black pepper, to taste
- 1½ tablespoons balsamic vinegar
- 60 ml rosemary, chopped
- 2 ribeye steaks

Instructions:
1. Melt the butter in a skillet over medium heat. Add the garlic and fry until fragrant.
2. Remove the skillet from the heat and add the salt, pepper, and vinegar. Allow it to cool.
3. Add the rosemary, then pour the mixture into a Ziploc bag.
4. Put the ribeye steaks in the bag and shake well, coating the meat well. Refrigerate for an hour, then allow to sit for a further twenty minutes.
5. Preheat the air fryer to 204°C.
6. Air fry the ribeye steaks for 15 minutes.
7. Take care when removing the steaks from the air fryer and plate up.
8. Serve immediately.

Cajun Bacon Pork Loin Fillet

Serves 6

Prep time: 30 minutes / Cook time: 20 minutes

Ingredients:
- 680 g pork loin fillet or pork tenderloin
- 3 tablespoons olive oil
- 2 tablespoons Cajun spice mix
- Salt, to taste
- 6 slices bacon
- Olive oil spray

Instructions:
1. Cut the pork in half so that it will fit in the air fryer basket.
2. Place both pieces of meat in a resealable plastic bag. Add the oil, Cajun seasoning, and salt to taste, if using. Seal the bag and massage to coat all of the meat with the oil and seasonings. Marinate in the refrigerator for at least 1 hour or up to 24 hours.
3. Remove the pork from the bag and wrap 3 bacon slices around each piece. Spray the air fryer basket with olive oil spray. Place the meat in the air fryer. Set the air fryer to 176°C for 15 minutes. Increase the temperature to 204°C for 5 minutes. Use a meat thermometer to ensure the meat has reached an internal temperature of 64°C.
4. Let the meat rest for 10 minutes. Slice into 6 medallions and serve.

Beef Whirls

Serves 6

Prep time: 30 minutes / Cook time: 18 minutes

Ingredients:
- 3 minute steaks (170 g each)
- 1 (450 g) bottle Italian dressing
- 235 ml Italian-style bread crumbs (or plain bread crumbs with Italian seasoning to taste)
- 120 ml grated Parmesan cheese
- 1 teaspoon dried basil
- 1 teaspoon dried oregano
- 1 teaspoon dried parsley

- 60 ml beef stock
- 1 to 2 tablespoons oil

Instructions:

1. In a large resealable bag, combine the steaks and Italian dressing. Seal the bag and refrigerate to marinate for 2 hours.
2. In a medium bowl, whisk the bread crumbs, cheese, basil, oregano, and parsley until blended. Stir in the beef stock.
3. Place the steaks on a cutting board and cut each in half so you have 6 equal pieces. Sprinkle with the bread crumb mixture. Roll up the steaks, jelly roll-style, and secure with toothpicks.
4. Preheat the air fryer to 204ºC.
5. Place 3 roll-ups in the air fryer basket.
6. Cook for 5 minutes. Flip the roll-ups and spritz with oil. Cook for 4 minutes more until the internal temperature reaches 64ºC. Repeat with the remaining roll-ups. Let rest for 5 to 10 minutes before serving.

Barbecue Ribs

Serves 4

Prep time: 5 minutes / Cook time: 30 minutes

Ingredients:

- 1 (900 g) rack baby back ribs
- 1 teaspoon onion granules
- 1 teaspoon garlic powder
- 1 teaspoon light brown sugar
- 1 teaspoon dried oregano
- Salt and freshly ground black pepper, to taste
- Cooking oil spray
- 120 ml barbecue sauce

Instructions:

1. Use a sharp knife to remove the thin membrane from the back of the ribs. Cut the rack in half, or as needed, so the ribs fit in the air fryer basket. The best way to do this is to cut the ribs into 4- or 5-rib sections.
2. In a small bowl, stir together the onion granules, garlic powder, brown sugar, and oregano and season with salt and pepper. Rub the spice seasoning onto the front and back of the ribs.
3. Cover the ribs with plastic wrap or foil and let sit at room temperature for 30 minutes.
4. Insert the crisper plate into the basket and the basket into the unit. Preheat the unit by selecting AIR ROAST, setting the temperature to 182ºC, and setting the time to 3 minutes. Select START/STOP to begin.
5. Once the unit is preheated, spray the crisper plate with cooking oil. Place the ribs into the basket. It is okay to stack them.
6. Select AIR ROAST, set the temperature to 182ºC, and set the time to 30 minutes. Select START/STOP to begin.
7. After 15 minutes, flip the ribs. Resume cooking for 15 minutes, or until a food thermometer registers 88ºC.
8. When the cooking is complete, transfer the ribs to a serving dish. Drizzle the ribs with the barbecue sauce and serve.

Pork Shoulder with Garlicky Coriander-Parsley Sauce

Serves 4

Prep time: 1 hour 15 minutes / Cook time: 30 minutes

Ingredients:

- 1 teaspoon flaxseed meal
- 1 egg white, well whisked
- 1 tablespoon soy sauce
- 1 teaspoon lemon juice, preferably freshly squeezed
- 1 tablespoon olive oil
- 450 g pork shoulder, cut into pieces 2-inches

long

- Salt and ground black pepper, to taste
- Garlicky Coriander-Parsley Sauce:
- 3 garlic cloves, minced
- 80 ml fresh coriander leaves
- 80 ml fresh parsley leaves
- 1 teaspoon lemon juice
- ½ tablespoon salt
- 80 ml extra-virgin olive oil

Instructions:

1. Combine the flaxseed meal, egg white, soy sauce, lemon juice, salt, black pepper, and olive oil in a large bowl. Dunk the pork strips in and press to submerge.
2. Wrap the bowl in plastic and refrigerate to marinate for at least an hour.
3. Preheat the air fryer to 192°C.
4. Arrange the marinated pork strips in the preheated air fryer and air fry for 30 minutes or until cooked through and well browned. Flip the strips halfway through.
5. Meanwhile, combine the ingredients for the sauce in a small bowl. Stir to mix well. Arrange the bowl in the refrigerator to chill until ready to serve.
6. Serve the air fried pork strips with the chilled sauce.

Steak, Broccoli, and Mushroom Rice Bowls

Serves 4

Prep time: 10 minutes / Cook time: 15 to 18 minutes

Ingredients:

- 2 tablespoons cornflour
- 120 ml low-sodium beef stock
- 1 teaspoon reduced-salt soy sauce
- 340 g rump steak, cut into 1-inch cubes
- 120 ml broccoli florets

- 1 onion, chopped
- 235 ml sliced white or chestnut mushrooms
- 1 tablespoon grated peeled fresh ginger
- Cooked brown rice (optional), for serving

Instructions:

1. In a medium bowl, stir together the cornflour, beef stock, and soy sauce until the cornflour is completely dissolved.
2. Add the beef cubes and toss to coat. Let stand for 5 minutes at room temperature.
3. Insert the crisper plate into the basket and the basket into the unit. Preheat the unit by selecting AIR FRY, setting the temperature to 204°C, and setting the time to 3 minutes. Select START/STOP to begin.
4. Once the unit is preheated, use a slotted spoon to transfer the beef from the stock mixture into a medium metal bowl that fits into the basket. Reserve the stock. Add the broccoli, onion, mushrooms, and ginger to the beef. Place the bowl into the basket.
5. Select AIR FRY, set the temperature to 204°C, and set the time to 18 minutes. Select START/STOP to begin.
6. After about 12 minutes, check the beef and broccoli. If a food thermometer inserted into the beef registers at least 64°C and the vegetables are tender, add the reserved stock and resume cooking for about 3 minutes until the sauce boils. If not, resume cooking for about 3 minutes before adding the reservedstock.
7. When the cooking is complete, serve immediately over hot cooked brown rice, if desired.

Super Bacon with Meat

Serves 4

Prep time: 5 minutes / Cook time: 1 hour

Ingredients:

- 30 slices thick-cut bacon
- 110 g Cheddar cheese, shredded
- 340 g steak
- 280 g pork sausage meat
- Salt and ground black pepper, to taste

Instructions:

1. Preheat the air fryer to 204ºC.
2. Lay out 30 slices of bacon in a woven pattern and bake for 20 minutes until crisp. Put the cheese in the center of the bacon.
3. Combine the steak and sausage to form a meaty mixture.
4. Lay out the meat in a rectangle of similar size to the bacon strips. Season with salt and pepper.
5. Roll the meat into a tight roll and refrigerate.
6. Preheat the air fryer to 204ºC.
7. Make a 7×7 bacon weave and roll the bacon weave over the meat, diagonally.
8. Bake for 60 minutes or until the internal temperature reaches at least 74ºC.
9. Let rest for 5 minutes before serving.

Reuben Beef Rolls with Thousand Island Sauce

Makes 10 rolls

Prep time: 15 minutes / Cook time: 10 minutes per batch

Ingredients:

- 230 g cooked salt beef, chopped
- 120 ml drained and chopped sauerkraut
- 1 (230 g) package cream cheese, softened
- 120 ml shredded Swiss cheese
- 20 slices prosciutto
- Cooking spray
- Thousand Island Sauce:
- 60 ml chopped dill pickles
- 60 ml tomato ketchup
- 180 ml mayonnaise
- Fresh thyme leaves, for garnish
- 2 tablespoons sugar
- ⅛ teaspoon fine sea salt
- Ground black pepper, to taste

Instructions:

1. Preheat the air fryer to 204ºC and spritz with cooking spray.
2. Combine the beef, sauerkraut, cream cheese, and Swiss cheese in a large bowl. Stir to mix well.
3. Unroll a slice of prosciutto on a clean work surface, then top with another slice of prosciutto crosswise. Scoop up 4 tablespoons of the beef mixture in the center.
4. Fold the top slice sides over the filling as the ends of the roll, then roll up the long sides of the bottom prosciutto and make it into a roll shape. Overlap the sides by about 1 inch. Repeat with remaining filling and prosciutto.
5. Arrange the rolls in the preheated air fryer, seam side down, and spritz with cooking spray.
6. Air fry for 10 minutes or until golden and crispy. Flip the rolls halfway through. Work in batches to avoid overcrowding.
7. Meanwhile, combine the ingredients for the sauce in a small bowl. Stir to mix well.
8. Serve the rolls with the dipping sauce.

Herbed Beef

Serves 6

Prep time: 5 minutes / Cook time: 22 minutes

Ingredients:

- 1 teaspoon dried dill
- 1 teaspoon dried thyme
- 1 teaspoon garlic powder
- 900 g beef steak
- 3 tablespoons butter

Instructions:

1. Preheat the air fryer to 182°C.
2. Combine the dill, thyme, and garlic powder in a small bowl, and massage into the steak.
3. Air fry the steak in the air fryer for 20 minutes, then remove, shred, and return to the air fryer.
4. Add the butter and air fry the shredded steak for a further 2 minutes at 185°C. Make sure the beef is coated in the butter before serving.

Blackened Steak Nuggets

Serves 2

Prep time: 10 minutes / Cook time: 7 minutes

Ingredients:

- 450 g rib eye steak, cut into 1-inch cubes
- 2 tablespoons salted butter, melted
- ½ teaspoon paprika
- ½ teaspoon salt
- ¼ teaspoon garlic powder
- ¼ teaspoon onion granules
- ¼ teaspoon ground black pepper
- ⅛ teaspoon cayenne pepper

Instructions:

1. Place steak into a large bowl and pour in butter. Toss to coat. Sprinkle with remaining ingredients.
2. Place bites into ungreased air fryer basket. Adjust the temperature to 204°C and air fry for 7 minutes, shaking the basket three times during cooking. Steak will be crispy on the outside and browned when done and internal temperature is at least 64°C for medium and 82°C for well-done. Serve warm.

Spicy Bavette Steak with Zhoug

Serves 4

Prep time: 30 minutes / Cook time: 8 minutes

Ingredients:

- Marinade and Steak:
- 120 ml dark beer or orange juice
- 60 ml fresh lemon juice
- 3 cloves garlic, minced
- 2 tablespoons extra-virgin olive oil
- 2 tablespoons Sriracha
- 2 tablespoons brown sugar
- 2 teaspoons ground cumin
- 2 teaspoons smoked paprika
- 1 tablespoon coarse or flaky salt
- 1 teaspoon black pepper
- 680 g bavette or skirt steak, trimmed and cut into 3 pieces
- Zhoug:
- 235 ml packed fresh coriander leaves
- 2 cloves garlic, peeled
- 2 jalapeño or green chiles, stemmed and coarsely chopped
- ½ teaspoon ground cumin
- ¼ teaspoon ground coriander
- ¼ teaspoon coarse or flaky salt
- 2 to 4 tablespoons extra-virgin olive oil

Instructions:

1. For the marinade and steak: In a small bowl, whisk together the beer, lemon juice, garlic, olive oil, Sriracha, brown sugar, cumin, paprika, salt, and pepper. Place the steak in a large resealable plastic bag. Pour the marinade over the steak, seal the bag, and massage the steak to coat. Marinate in the refrigerator for 1 hour or up to 24 hours, turning the bag occasionally.
2. Meanwhile, for the zhoug: In a food processor, combine the coriander, garlic, jalapeños, cumin, coriander, and salt. Process

until finely chopped. Add 2 tablespoons olive oil and pulse to form a loose paste, adding up to 2 tablespoons more olive oil if needed. Transfer the zhoug to a glass container. Cover and store in the refrigerator until 30 minutes before serving if marinating more than 1 hour.

3. Remove the steak from the marinade and discard the marinade. Place the steak in the air fryer basket and set the air fryer to 204°C for 8 minutes. Use a meat thermometer to ensure the steak has reached an internal temperature of 64°C (for medium).

4. Transfer the steak to a cutting board and let rest for 5 minutes. Slice the steak across the grain and serve with the zhoug.

Goat Cheese-Stuffed Bavette Steak

Serves 6

Prep time: 10 minutes / Cook time: 14 minutes

Ingredients:

- 450 g bavette or skirt steak
- 1 tablespoon avocado oil
- ½ teaspoon sea salt
- ½ teaspoon garlic powder
- ¼ teaspoon freshly ground black pepper
- 60 g goat cheese, crumbled
- 235 ml baby spinach, chopped

Instructions:

1. Place the steak in a large zip-top bag or between two pieces of plastic wrap. Using a meat mallet or heavy-bottomed skillet, pound the steak to an even ¼-inch thickness.

2. Brush both sides of the steak with the avocado oil.

3. Mix the salt, garlic powder, and pepper in a small dish. Sprinkle this mixture over both

sides of the steak.

4. Sprinkle the goat cheese over top, and top that with the spinach.

5. Starting at one of the long sides, roll the steak up tightly. Tie the rolled steak with kitchen string at 3-inch intervals.

6. Set the air fryer to 204°C. Place the steak roll-up in the air fryer basket. Air fry for 7 minutes. Flip the steak and cook for an additional 7 minutes, until an instant-read thermometer reads 49°C for medium-rare (adjust the cooking time for your desired doneness).

Indian Mint and Chile Kebabs

Serves 4

Prep time: 30 minutes / Cook time: 15 minutes

Ingredients:

- 450 g lamb mince
- 120 ml finely minced onion
- 60 ml chopped fresh mint
- 60 ml chopped fresh coriander
- 1 tablespoon minced garlic
- ½ teaspoon ground turmeric
- ½ teaspoon cayenne pepper
- ¼ teaspoon ground cardamom
- ¼ teaspoon ground cinnamon
- 1 teaspoon coarse or flaky salt

Instructions:

1. In the bowl of a stand mixer fitted with the paddle attachment, combine the lamb, onion, mint, coriander, garlic, turmeric, cayenne, cardamom, cinnamon, and salt. Mix on low speed until you have a sticky mess of spiced meat. If you have time, let the mixture stand at room temperature for 30 minutes (or cover and refrigerate for up to a day or two, until you're ready to make the kebabs).

2. Divide the meat into eight equal portions.

Form each into a long sausage shape. Place the kebabs in a single layer in the air fryer basket. Set the air fryer to 176°C for 10 minutes. Increase the air fryer temperature to 204°C and cook for 3 to 4 minutes more to brown the kebabs. Use a meat thermometer to ensure the kebabs have reached an internal temperature of 72°C (medium).

Beef Bavette Steak with Sage

Serves 2

Prep time: 13 minutes / Cook time: 7 minutes

Ingredients:
- 80 ml sour cream
- 120 ml spring onion, chopped
- 1 tablespoon mayonnaise
- 3 cloves garlic, smashed
- 450 g beef bavette or skirt steak, trimmed and cubed
- 2 tablespoons fresh sage, minced
- ½ teaspoon salt
- ⅓ teaspoon black pepper, or to taste

Instructions:
1. Season your meat with salt and pepper; arrange beef cubes on the bottom of a baking dish that fits in your air fryer.
2. Stir in spring onions and garlic; air fry for about 7 minutes at 196°C.
3. Once your beef starts to tender, add the cream, mayonnaise, and sage; air fry an additional 8 minutes. Bon appétit!

Bean and Beef Meatball Taco Pizza

Serves 4

Prep time: 10 minutes / Cook time: 7 to 9 minutes per batch

Ingredients:
- 180 ml refried beans (from a 450 g can)
- 120 ml salsa
- 10 frozen precooked beef meatballs, thawed and sliced
- 1 jalapeño pepper, sliced
- 4 whole-wheat pitta breads
- 235 ml shredded chilli cheese
- 120 ml shredded Monterey Jack or Cheddar cheese
- Cooking oil spray
- 80 ml sour cream

Instructions:
1. In a medium bowl, stir together the refried beans, salsa, meatballs, and jalapeño.
2. Insert the crisper plate into the basket and the basket into the unit. Preheat the unit by selecting BAKE, setting the temperature to 192°C, and setting the time to 3 minutes. Select START/STOP to begin.
3. Top the pittas with the refried bean mixture and sprinkle with the cheeses.
4. Once the unit is preheated, spray the crisper plate with cooking oil. Working in batches, place the pizzas into the basket. Select BAKE, set the temperature to 192°C, and set the time to 9 minutes. Select START/STOP to begin.
5. After about 7 minutes, check the pizzas. They are done when the cheese is melted and starts to brown. If not ready, resume cooking.
6. When the cooking is complete, top each pizza with a dollop of sour cream and serve warm.

Lamb Burger with Feta and Olives

Serves 3 to 4

Prep time: 10 minutes / Cook time: 20 minutes

Ingredients:

- 2 teaspoons olive oil
- ⅓ onion, finely chopped
- 1 clove garlic, minced
- 450 g lamb mince
- 2 tablespoons fresh parsley, finely chopped
- 1½ teaspoons fresh oregano, finely chopped
- 120 ml black olives, finely chopped
- 80 ml crumbled feta cheese
- ½ teaspoon salt
- Freshly ground black pepper, to taste
- 4 thick pitta breads

Instructions:

1. Preheat a medium skillet over medium-high heat on the stovetop. Add the olive oil and cook the onion until tender, but not browned, about 4 to 5 minutes. Add the garlic and cook for another minute. Transfer the onion and garlic to a mixing bowl and add the lamb mince, parsley, oregano, olives, feta cheese, salt and pepper. Gently mix the ingredients together.
2. Divide the mixture into 3 or 4 equal portions and then form the hamburgers, being careful not to over-handle the meat. One good way to do this is to throw the meat back and forth between your hands like a baseball, packing the meat each time you catch it. Flatten the balls into patties, making an indentation in the center of each patty. Flatten the sides of the patties as well to make it easier to fit them into the air fryer basket.
3. Preheat the air fryer to 188ºC.
4. If you don't have room for all four burgers, air fry two or three burgers at a time for 8 minutes at 188ºC. Flip the burgers over and air fry for another 8 minutes. If you cooked your burgers in batches, return the first batch of burgers to the air fryer for the last two minutes of cooking to re-heat. This should give you a medium-well burger. If you'd prefer a medium-rare burger, shorten the cooking time to about 13 minutes. Remove the burgers to a resting plate and let the burgers rest for a few minutes before dressing and serving.
5. While the burgers are resting, toast the pitta breads in the air fryer for 2 minutes. Tuck the burgers into the toasted pitta breads, or wrap the pittas around the burgers and serve with a tzatziki sauce or some mayonnaise.

Spice-Rubbed Pork Loin

Serves 6

Prep time: 5 minutes / Cook time: 20 minutes

Ingredients:

- 1 teaspoon paprika
- ½ teaspoon ground cumin
- ½ teaspoon chili powder
- ½ teaspoon garlic powder
- 2 tablespoons coconut oil
- 1 (680 g) boneless pork loin
- ½ teaspoon salt
- ¼ teaspoon ground black pepper

Instructions:

1. In a small bowl, mix paprika, cumin, chili powder, and garlic powder.
2. Drizzle coconut oil over pork. Sprinkle pork loin with salt and pepper, then rub spice mixture evenly on all sides.
3. Place pork loin into ungreased air fryer basket. Adjust the temperature to 204ºC and air fry for 20 minutes, turning pork halfway through cooking. Pork loin will be browned

and have an internal temperature of at least 64ºC when done. Serve warm.

Herbed Lamb Steaks

Serves 4

Prep time: 30 minutes / Cook time: 15 minutes

Ingredients:

- ½ medium onion
- 2 tablespoons minced garlic
- 2 teaspoons ground ginger
- 1 teaspoon ground cinnamon
- 1 teaspoon onion granules
- 1 teaspoon cayenne pepper
- 1 teaspoon salt
- 4 (170 g) boneless lamb sirloin steaks
- Oil, for spraying

Instructions:

1. In a blender, combine the onion, garlic, ginger, cinnamon, onion granules, cayenne pepper, and salt and pulse until the onion is minced.
2. Place the lamb steaks in a large bowl or zip-top plastic bag and sprinkle the onion mixture over the top. Turn the steaks until they are evenly coated. Cover with plastic wrap or seal the bag and refrigerate for 30 minutes.
3. Preheat the air fryer to 164ºC. Line the air fryer basket with parchment and spray lightly with oil.
4. Place the lamb steaks in a single layer in the prepared basket, making sure they don't overlap. You may need to work in batches, depending on the size of your air fryer.
5. Cook for 8 minutes, flip, and cook for another 7 minutes, or until the internal temperature reaches 68ºC.

Pork Bulgogi

Serves 4

Prep time: 30 minutes / Cook time: 15 minutes

Ingredients:

- 1 onion, thinly sliced
- 2 tablespoons gochujang (Korean red chili paste)
- 1 tablespoon minced fresh ginger
- 1 tablespoon minced garlic
- 1 tablespoon soy sauce
- 1 tablespoon Shaoxing wine (rice cooking wine)
- 1 tablespoon toasted sesame oil
- 1 teaspoon sugar
- ¼ to 1 teaspoon cayenne pepper or gochugaru (Korean ground red pepper)
- 450 g boneless pork shoulder, cut into ½-inch-thick slices
- 1 tablespoon sesame seeds
- 60 ml sliced spring onionspring onions

Instructions:

1. In a large bowl, combine the onion, gochujang, ginger, garlic, soy sauce, wine, sesame oil, sugar, and cayenne. Add the pork and toss to coat. Marinate at room temperature for 30 minutes, or cover and refrigerate for up to 24 hours.
2. Arrange the pork and onion slices in the air fryer basket; discard the marinade. Set the air fryer to 204ºC for 15 minutes, turning the pork halfway through the cooking time.
3. Arrange the pork on a serving platter. Sprinkle with the sesame seeds and spring onionspring onions and serve.

CHAPTER 6 VEGETABLES AND SIDES

Garlic Courgette and Red Peppers

Serves 6

Prep time: 5 minutes / Cook time: 15 minutes

Ingredients:
- 2 medium courgette, cubed
- 1 red pepper, diced
- 2 garlic cloves, sliced
- 2 tablespoons olive oil
- ½ teaspoon salt

Instructions:
1. Preheat the air fryer to 193ºC.
2. In a large bowl, mix together the courgette, bell pepper, and garlic with the olive oil and salt.
3. Pour the mixture into the air fryer basket, and roast for 7 minutes. Shake or stir, then roast for 7 to 8 minutes more.

Mushrooms with Goat Cheese

Serves 4

Prep time: 10 minutes / Cook time: 10 minutes

Ingredients:
- 3 tablespoons vegetable oil
- 450 g mixed mushrooms, trimmed and sliced
- 1 clove garlic, minced
- ¼ teaspoon dried thyme
- ½ teaspoon black pepper
- 110 g goat cheese, diced
- 2 teaspoons chopped fresh thyme leaves (optional)

Instructions:
1. In a baking pan, combine the oil, mushrooms, garlic, dried thyme, and pepper. Stir in the goat cheese. Place the pan in the air fryer basket. Set the air fryer to 200ºC for 10 minutes, stirring halfway through the cooking time.
2. Sprinkle with fresh thyme, if desired.

Parmesan Herb Focaccia Bread

Serves 6

Prep time: 10 minutes / Cook time: 10 minutes

Ingredients:
- 225 g shredded Mozzarella cheese
- 30 g) full-fat cream cheese
- 95 g blanched finely ground almond flour
- 40 g ground golden flaxseed
- 20 g grated Parmesan cheese
- ½ teaspoon bicarbonate of soda
- 2 large eggs
- ½ teaspoon garlic powder
- ¼ teaspoon dried basil
- ¼ teaspoon dried rosemary
- 2 tablespoons salted butter, melted and divided

Instructions:
1. Place Mozzarella, cream cheese, and almond flour into a large microwave-safe bowl and microwave for 1 minute. Add the flaxseed, Parmesan, and bicarbonate of soda and stir until smooth ball forms. If the mixture cools too much, it will be hard to mix. Return to microwave for 10 to 15 seconds to rewarm if necessary.
2. Stir in eggs. You may need to use your hands to get them fully incorporated. Just keep stirring and they will absorb into the dough.
3. Sprinkle dough with garlic powder, basil, and rosemary and knead into dough. Grease a baking pan with 1 tablespoon melted butter. Press the dough evenly into the pan. Place pan into the air fryer basket.
4. Adjust the temperature to 200ºC and bake for 10 minutes.

5. At 7 minutes, cover with foil if bread begins to get too dark.
6. Remove and let cool at least 30 minutes. Drizzle with remaining butter and serve.

Courgette Fritters

Serves 4

Prep time: 10 minutes / Cook time: 10 minutes

Ingredients:

- 2 courgette, grated (about 450 g)
- 1 teaspoon salt
- 25 g almond flour
- 20 g grated Parmesan cheese
- 1 large egg
- ¼ teaspoon dried thyme
- ¼ teaspoon ground turmeric
- ¼ teaspoon freshly ground black pepper
- 1 tablespoon olive oil
- ½ lemon, sliced into wedges

Instructions:

1. Preheat the air fryer to 200°C. Cut a piece of parchment paper to fit slightly smaller than the bottom of the air fryer.
2. Place the courgette in a large colander and sprinkle with the salt. Let sit for 5 to 10 minutes. Squeeze as much liquid as you can from the courgette and place in a large mixing bowl. Add the almond flour, Parmesan, egg, thyme, turmeric, and black pepper. Stir gently until thoroughly combined.
3. Shape the mixture into 8 patties and arrange on the parchment paper. Brush lightly with the olive oil. Pausing halfway through the cooking time to turn the patties, air fry for 10 minutes until golden brown. Serve warm with the lemon wedges.

Sausage-Stuffed Mushroom Caps

Serves 2

Prep time: 10 minutes / Cook time: 8 minutes

Ingredients:

- 6 large portobello mushroom caps
- 230 g Italian sausage
- 15 g chopped onion
- 2 tablespoons blanched finely ground almond flour
- 20 g grated Parmesan cheese
- 1 teaspoon minced fresh garlic

Instructions:

1. Use a spoon to hollow out each mushroom cap, reserving scrapings.
2. In a medium skillet over medium heat, brown the sausage about 10 minutes or until fully cooked and no pink remains. Drain and then add reserved mushroom scrapings, onion, almond flour, Parmesan, and garlic. Gently fold ingredients together and continue cooking an additional minute, then remove from heat.
3. Evenly spoon the mixture into mushroom caps and place the caps into a 6-inch round pan. Place pan into the air fryer basket.
4. Adjust the temperature to 192°C and set the timer for 8 minutes.
5. When finished cooking, the tops will be browned and bubbling. Serve warm.

Tofu Bites

Serves 4

Prep time: 15 minutes / Cook time: 30 minutes

Ingredients:

- 1 packaged firm tofu, cubed and pressed to remove excess water
- 1 tablespoon soy sauce
- 1 tablespoon ketchup
- 1 tablespoon maple syrup

- ½ teaspoon vinegar
- 1 teaspoon liquid smoke
- 1 teaspoon hot sauce
- 2 tablespoons sesame seeds
- 1 teaspoon garlic powder
- Salt and ground black pepper, to taste
- Cooking spray

Instructions:

1. Preheat the air fryer to 192°C.
2. Spritz a baking dish with cooking spray.
3. Combine all the ingredients to coat the tofu completely and allow the marinade to absorb for half an hour.
4. Transfer the tofu to the baking dish, then air fry for 15 minutes. Flip the tofu over and air fry for another 15 minutes on the other side.
5. Serve immediately.

Saltine Wax Beans

Serves 4

Prep time: 10 minutes / Cook time: 7 minutes

Ingredients:

- 60 g flour
- 1 teaspoon smoky chipotle powder
- ½ teaspoon ground black pepper
- 1 teaspoon sea salt flakes
- 2 eggs, beaten
- 55 g crushed cream crackers
- 285 g wax beans
- Cooking spray

Instructions:

1. Preheat the air fryer to 180°C.
2. Combine the flour, chipotle powder, black pepper, and salt in a bowl. Put the eggs in a second bowl. Put the crushed cream crackers in a third bowl.
3. Wash the beans with cold water and discard any tough strings.
4. Coat the beans with the flour mixture, before

dipping them into the beaten egg. Cover them with the crushed cream crackers.
5. Spritz the beans with cooking spray.
6. Air fry for 4 minutes. Give the air fryer basket a good shake and continue to air fry for 3 minutes. Serve hot.

Curry Roasted Cauliflower

Serves 4

Prep time: 10 minutes / Cook time: 20 minutes

Ingredients:

- 65 ml olive oil
- 2 teaspoons curry powder
- ½ teaspoon salt
- ¼ teaspoon freshly ground black pepper
- 1 head cauliflower, cut into bite-size florets
- ½ red onion, sliced
- 2 tablespoons freshly chopped parsley, for garnish (optional)

Instructions:

1. Preheat the air fryer to 200°C.
2. In a large bowl, combine the olive oil, curry powder, salt, and pepper. Add the cauliflower and onion. Toss gently until the vegetables are completely coated with the oil mixture. Transfer the vegetables to the basket of the air fryer.
3. Pausing about halfway through the cooking time to shake the basket, air fry for 20 minutes until the cauliflower is tender and beginning to brown. Top with the parsley, if desired, before serving.

Flatbread

Serves 2

Prep time: 5 minutes / Cook time: 7 minutes

Ingredients:

- 225 g shredded Mozzarella cheese
- 25 g blanched finely ground almond flour

- 30 g full-fat cream cheese, softened

Instructions:

1. In a large microwave-safe bowl, melt Mozzarella in the microwave for 30 seconds. Stir in almond flour until smooth and then add cream cheese. Continue mixing until dough forms, gently kneading it with wet hands if necessary.
2. Divide the dough into two pieces and roll out to ¼-inch thickness between two pieces of parchment. Cut another piece of parchment to fit your air fryer basket.
3. Place a piece of flatbread onto your parchment and into the air fryer, working in two batches if needed.
4. Adjust the temperature to 160°C and air fry for 7 minutes.
5. Halfway through the cooking time flip the flatbread. Serve warm.

Creamed Asparagus

Serves 4

Prep time: 10 minutes / Cook time: 18 minutes

Ingredients:

- 120 g whipping cream
- 45 g grated Parmesan cheese
- 60 g cream cheese, softened
- 450 g asparagus, ends trimmed, chopped into 1-inch pieces
- ¼ teaspoon salt
- ¼ teaspoon ground black pepper

Instructions:

1. In a medium bowl, whisk together whipping cream, Parmesan, and cream cheese until combined.
2. Place asparagus into an ungreased round nonstick baking dish. Pour cheese mixture over top and sprinkle with salt and pepper.
3. Place dish into air fryer basket. Adjust the

temperature to 180°C and set the timer for 18 minutes. Asparagus will be tender when done. Serve warm.

Asian Tofu Salad

Serves 2

Prep time: 25 minutes / Cook time: 15 minutes

Ingredients:

Tofu:
- 1 tablespoon soy sauce
- 1 tablespoon vegetable oil
- 1 teaspoon minced fresh ginger
- 1 teaspoon minced garlic
- 230 g extra-firm tofu, drained and cubed

Salad:
- 60 ml rice vinegar
- 1 tablespoon sugar
- 1 teaspoon salt
- 1 teaspoon black pepper
- 25 g sliced spring onions
- 120 g julienned cucumber
- 50 g julienned red onion
- 130 g julienned carrots
- 6 butter lettuce leaves

Instructions:

1. For the tofu: In a small bowl, whisk together the soy sauce, vegetable oil, ginger, and garlic. Add the tofu and mix gently. Let stand at room temperature for 10 minutes.
2. Arrange the tofu in a single layer in the air fryer basket. Set the air fryer to 200°C for 15 minutes, shaking halfway through the cooking time.
3. Meanwhile, for the salad: In a large bowl, whisk together the vinegar, sugar, salt, pepper, and spring onions. Add the cucumber, onion, and carrots and toss to combine. Set aside to marinate while the tofu cooks.
4. To serve, arrange three lettuce leaves on each of two plates. Pile the marinated vegetables

(and marinade) on the lettuce. Divide the tofu between the plates and serve.

Baked Jalapeño and Cheese Cauliflower Mash

Serves 6

Prep time: 10 minutes / Cook time: 15 minutes

Ingredients:

- 1 (340 g) steamer bag cauliflower florets, cooked according to package instructions
- 2 tablespoons salted butter, softened
- 60 g cream cheese, softened
- 120 g shredded sharp Cheddar cheese
- 20 g pickled jalapeños
- ½ teaspoon salt
- ¼ teaspoon ground black pepper

Instructions:

1. Place cooked cauliflower into a food processor with remaining ingredients. Pulse twenty times until cauliflower is smooth and all ingredients are combined.
2. Spoon mash into an ungreased round nonstick baking dish. Place dish into air fryer basket. Adjust the temperature to 192°C and bake for 15 minutes. The top will be golden brown when done. Serve warm.

Rosemary New Potatoes

Serves 4

Prep time: 10 minutes / Cook time: 5 to 6 minutes

Ingredients:

- 3 large red potatoes
- ¼ teaspoon ground rosemary
- ¼ teaspoon ground thyme
- ⅛ teaspoon salt
- ⅛ teaspoon ground black pepper
- 2 teaspoons extra-light olive oil

Instructions:

1. Preheat the air fryer to 170°C. 2. Place potatoes in large bowl and sprinkle with rosemary, thyme, salt, and pepper.
3. Stir with a spoon to distribute seasonings evenly.
4. Add oil to potatoes and stir again to coat well.
5. Air fry at 170°C for 4 minutes. Stir and break apart any that have stuck together.
6. Cook an additional 1 to 2 minutes or until fork-tender.

Cauliflower Steaks Gratin

Serves 2

Prep time: 10 minutes / Cook time: 13 minutes

Ingredients:

- 1 head cauliflower
- 1 tablespoon olive oil
- Salt and freshly ground black pepper, to taste
- ½ teaspoon chopped fresh thyme leaves
- 3 tablespoons grated Parmigiano-Reggiano cheese
- 2 tablespoons panko bread crumbs

Instructions:

1. Preheat the air fryer to 192°C.
2. Cut two steaks out of the centre of the cauliflower. To do this, cut the cauliflower in half and then cut one slice about 1-inch thick off each half. The rest of the cauliflower will fall apart into florets, which you can roast on their own or save for another meal.
3. Brush both sides of the cauliflower steaks with olive oil and season with salt, freshly ground black pepper and fresh thyme. Place the cauliflower steaks into the air fryer basket and air fry for 6 minutes. Turn the steaks over and air fry for another 4 minutes. Combine the Parmesan cheese and panko bread crumbs and sprinkle the mixture over

the tops of both steaks and air fry for another 3 minutes until the cheese has melted and the bread crumbs have browned. Serve this with some sautéed bitter greens and air-fried blistered tomatoes.

Blistered Shishito Peppers with Lime Juice

Serves 3

Prep time: 5 minutes / Cook time: 9 minutes

Ingredients:
- 230 g shishito peppers, rinsed
- Cooking spray
- Sauce:
- 1 tablespoon tamari or shoyu
- 2 teaspoons fresh lime juice
- 2 large garlic cloves, minced

Instructions:
1. Preheat the air fryer to 200°C. Spritz the air fryer basket with cooking spray.
2. Place the shishito peppers in the basket and spritz them with cooking spray. Roast for 3 minutes.
3. Meanwhile, whisk together all the ingredients for the sauce in a large bowl. Set aside.
4. Shake the basket and spritz them with cooking spray again, then roast for an additional 3 minutes.
5. Shake the basket one more time and spray the peppers with cooking spray. Continue roasting for 3 minutes until the peppers are blistered and nicely browned.
6. Remove the peppers from the basket to the bowl of sauce. Toss to coat well and serve immediately.

Citrus Sweet Potatoes and Carrots

Serves 4

Prep time: 5 minutes / Cook time: 20 to 25 minutes

Ingredients:
- 2 large carrots, cut into 1-inch chunks
- 1 medium sweet potato, peeled and cut into 1-inch cubes
- 25 g chopped onion
- 2 garlic cloves, minced
- 2 tablespoons honey
- 1 tablespoon freshly squeezed orange juice
- 2 teaspoons butter, melted

Instructions:
1. Insert the crisper plate into the basket and the basket into the unit. Preheat the unit by selecting AIR ROAST, setting the temperature to 200°C, and setting the time to 3 minutes. Select START/STOP to begin.
2. In a 6-by-2-inch round pan, toss together the carrots, sweet potato, onion, garlic, honey, orange juice, and melted butter to coat.
3. Once the unit is preheated, place the pan into the basket.
4. Select AIR ROAST, set the temperature to 200°C, and set the time to 25 minutes. Select START/STOP to begin.
5. After 15 minutes, remove the basket and shake the vegetables. Reinsert the basket to resume cooking. After 5 minutes, if the vegetables are tender and glazed, they are done. If not, resume cooking.
6. When the cooking is complete, serve immediately.

"Faux-Tato" Hash

Serves 4

Prep time: 10 minutes / Cook time: 12 minutes

Ingredients:
- 450 g radishes, ends removed, quartered
- ¼ medium yellow onion, peeled and diced
- ½ medium green pepper, seeded and chopped
- 2 tablespoons salted butter, melted

- ½ teaspoon garlic powder
- ¼ teaspoon ground black pepper

Instructions:

1. In a large bowl, combine radishes, onion, and bell pepper. Toss with butter.
2. Sprinkle garlic powder and black pepper over mixture in bowl, then spoon into ungreased air fryer basket.
3. Adjust the temperature to 160ºC and air fry for 12 minutes. Shake basket halfway through cooking. Radishes will be tender when done. Serve warm.

Gorgonzola Mushrooms with Horseradish Mayo

Serves 5

Prep time: 15 minutes / Cook time: 10 minutes

Ingredients:

- 60 g bread crumbs
- 2 cloves garlic, pressed
- 2 tablespoons chopped fresh coriander
- ⅓ teaspoon coarse sea salt
- ½ teaspoon crushed red pepper flakes
- 1½ tablespoons olive oil
- 20 medium mushrooms, stems removed
- 55 g grated Gorgonzola cheese
- 55 g low-fat mayonnaise
- 1 teaspoon prepared horseradish, well-drained
- 1 tablespoon finely chopped fresh parsley

Instructions:

1. Preheat the air fryer to 192ºC.
2. Combine the bread crumbs together with the garlic, coriander, salt, red pepper, and olive oil.
3. Take equal-sized amounts of the bread crumb mixture and use them to stuff the mushroom caps. Add the grated Gorgonzola on top of each.
4. Put the mushrooms in a baking pan and transfer to the air fryer.
5. Air fry for 10 minutes, ensuring the stuffing is warm throughout.
6. In the meantime, prepare the horseradish mayo. Mix the mayonnaise, horseradish and parsley.
7. When the mushrooms are ready, serve with the mayo.

Mediterranean Courgette Boats

Serves 4

Prep time: 5 minutes / Cook time: 10 minutes

Ingredients:

- 1 large courgette, ends removed, halved lengthwise
- 6 grape tomatoes, quartered
- ¼ teaspoon salt
- 65 g feta cheese
- 1 tablespoon balsamic vinegar
- 1 tablespoon olive oil

Instructions:

1. Use a spoon to scoop out 2 tablespoons from centre of each courgette half, making just enough space to fill with tomatoes and feta.
2. Place tomatoes evenly in centres of courgette halves and sprinkle with salt. Place into ungreased air fryer basket. Adjust the temperature to 180ºC and roast for 10 minutes. When done, courgette will be tender.
3. Transfer boats to a serving tray and sprinkle with feta, then drizzle with vinegar and olive oil. Serve warm.

Mashed Sweet Potato Tots

Makes 18 to 24 tots

Prep time: 10 minutes / Cook time: 12 to 13 minutes per batch

Ingredients:

- 210 g cooked mashed sweet potatoes

- 1 egg white, beaten
- ⅛ teaspoon ground cinnamon
- 1 dash nutmeg
- 2 tablespoons chopped pecans
- 1½ teaspoons honey
- Salt, to taste
- 50 g panko bread crumbs
- Oil for misting or cooking spray

Instructions:

1. Preheat the air fryer to 200°C.
2. In a large bowl, mix together the potatoes, egg white, cinnamon, nutmeg, pecans, honey, and salt to taste.
3. Place panko crumbs on a sheet of wax paper.
4. For each tot, use about 2 teaspoons of sweet potato mixture. To shape, drop the measure of potato mixture onto panko crumbs and push crumbs up and around potatoes to coat edges. Then turn tot over to coat other side with crumbs.
5. Mist tots with oil or cooking spray and place in air fryer basket in single layer.
6. Air fry at 200°C for 12 to 13 minutes, until browned and crispy.
7. Repeat steps 5 and 6 to cook remaining tots.

Easy Rosemary Green Beans

Serves 1

Prep time: 5 minutes / Cook time: 5 minutes

Ingredients:

- 1 tablespoon butter, melted
- 2 tablespoons rosemary
- ½ teaspoon salt
- 3 cloves garlic, minced
- 95 g chopped green beans

Instructions:

1. Preheat the air fryer to 200°C.
2. Combine the melted butter with the rosemary, salt, and minced garlic. Toss in the green beans, coating them well.
3. Air fry for 5 minutes.
4. Serve immediately.

Fig, Chickpea, and Rocket Salad

Serves 4

Prep time: 15 minutes / Cook time: 20 minutes

Ingredients:

- 8 fresh figs, halved
- 250 g cooked chickpeas
- 1 teaspoon crushed roasted cumin seeds
- 4 tablespoons balsamic vinegar
- 2 tablespoons extra-virgin olive oil, plus more for greasing
- Salt and ground black pepper, to taste
- 40 g rocket, washed and dried

Instructions:

1. Preheat the air fryer to 192°C.
2. Cover the air fryer basket with aluminum foil and grease lightly with oil. Put the figs in the air fryer basket and air fry for 10 minutes.
3. In a bowl, combine the chickpeas and cumin seeds.
4. Remove the air fried figs from the air fryer and replace with the chickpeas. Air fry for 10 minutes. Leave to cool.
5. In the meantime, prepare the dressing. Mix the balsamic vinegar, olive oil, salt and pepper.
6. In a salad bowl, combine the rocket with the cooled figs and chickpeas.
7. Toss with the sauce and serve.

Brussels Sprouts with Pecans and Gorgonzola

Serves 4

Prep time: 10 minutes / Cook time: 25 minutes

Ingredients:

- 65 g pecans

- 680 g fresh Brussels sprouts, trimmed and quartered
- 2 tablespoons olive oil
- Salt and freshly ground black pepper, to taste
- 30 g crumbled Gorgonzola cheese

Instructions:

1. Spread the pecans in a single layer of the air fryer and set the heat to 180ºC. Air fry for 3 to 5 minutes until the pecans are lightly browned and fragrant. Transfer the pecans to a plate and continue preheating the air fryer, increasing the heat to 200ºC.
2. In a large bowl, toss the Brussels sprouts with the olive oil and season with salt and black pepper to taste.
3. Working in batches if necessary, arrange the Brussels sprouts in a single layer in the air fryer basket. Pausing halfway through the baking time to shake the basket, air fry for 20 to 25 minutes until the sprouts are tender and starting to brown on the edges.
4. Transfer the sprouts to a serving bowl and top with the toasted pecans and Gorgonzola. Serve warm or at room temperature.

Cauliflower Rice Balls

Serves 4

Prep time: 10 minutes / Cook time: 8 minutes

Ingredients:

- 1 (280 g) steamer bag cauliflower rice, cooked according to package instructions
- 110 g shredded Mozzarella cheese
- 1 large egg
- 60 g plain pork scratchings, finely crushed
- ¼ teaspoon salt
- ½ teaspoon Italian seasoning

Instructions:

1. Place cauliflower into a large bowl and mix with Mozzarella.
2. Whisk egg in a separate medium bowl. Place

pork scratchings into another large bowl with salt and Italian seasoning.
3. Separate cauliflower mixture into four equal sections and form each into a ball. Carefully dip a ball into whisked egg, then roll in pork scratchings. Repeat with remaining balls.
4. Place cauliflower balls into ungreased air fryer basket. Adjust the temperature to 200ºC and air fry for 8 minutes. Rice balls will be golden when done.
5. Use a spatula to carefully move cauliflower balls to a large dish for serving. Serve warm.

Crispy Lemon Artichoke Hearts

Serves 2

Prep time: 10 minutes / Cook time: 15 minutes

Ingredients:

- 1 (425 g) can artichoke hearts in water, drained
- 1 egg
- 1 tablespoon water
- 30 g whole wheat bread crumbs
- ¼ teaspoon salt
- ¼ teaspoon paprika
- ½ lemon

Instructions:

1. Preheat the air fryer to 192ºC.
2. In a medium shallow bowl, beat together the egg and water until frothy.
3. In a separate medium shallow bowl, mix together the bread crumbs, salt, and paprika.
4. Dip each artichoke heart into the egg mixture, then into the bread crumb mixture, coating the outside with the crumbs. Place the artichokes hearts in a single layer of the air fryer basket.
5. Fry the artichoke hearts for 15 minutes.
6. Remove the artichokes from the air fryer, and squeeze fresh lemon juice over the top before serving.

CHAPTER 7 VEGETARIAN MAINS

Crustless Spinach Cheese Pie

Serves 4

Prep time: 10 minutes / Cook time: 20 minutes

Ingredients:

- 6 large eggs
- 60 ml double cream
- 235 ml frozen chopped spinach, drained
- 235 ml shredded sharp Cheddar cheese
- 60 ml diced brown onion

Instructions:

1. In a medium bowl, whisk eggs and add cream.
2. Add remaining ingredients to bowl. Pour into a round baking dish.
3. Place into the air fryer basket. Adjust the temperature to 160°C and bake for 20 minutes.
4. Eggs will be firm and slightly browned when cooked.
5. Serve immediately.

Super Veg Rolls

Serves 6

Prep time: 20 minutes / Cook time: 10 minutes

Ingredients:

- 2 potatoes, mashed
- 60 ml peas
- 60 ml mashed carrots
- 1 small cabbage, sliced
- 60 ml beans
- 2 tablespoons sweetcorn
- 1 small onion, chopped
- 120 ml breadcrumbs
- 1 packet spring roll sheets

- 120 ml cornflour slurry (mix 40 ml cornflour with 80 ml water)

Instructions:

1. Preheat the air fryer to 200°C.
2. Boil all the vegetables in water over a low heat.
3. Rinse and allow to dry. Unroll the spring roll sheets and spoon equal amounts of vegetable onto the centre of each one.
4. Fold into spring rolls and coat each one with the slurry and breadcrumbs.
5. Air fry the rolls in the preheated air fryer for 10 minutes.
6. Serve warm.

Spaghetti Squash Alfredo

Serves 2

Prep time: 10 minutes / Cook time: 15 minutes

Ingredients:

- ½ large cooked spaghetti squash
- 2 tablespoons salted butter, melted
- 120 ml low-carb Alfredo sauce
- 60 ml grated vegetarian Parmesan cheese
- ½ teaspoon garlic powder
- 1 teaspoon dried parsley
- ¼ teaspoon ground peppercorn
- 120 ml shredded Italian blend cheese

Instructions:

1. Using a fork, remove the strands of spaghetti squash from the shell.
2. Place into a large bowl with butter and Alfredo sauce.
3. Sprinkle with Parmesan, garlic powder, parsley, and peppercorn.
4. Pour into a 1 L round baking dish and top with shredded cheese.

5. Place dish into the air fryer basket.
6. Adjust the temperature to 160ºC and bake for 15 minutes.
7. When finished, cheese will be golden and bubbling.
8. Serve immediately.

Mediterranean Pan Pizza

Serves 2

Prep time: 5 minutes / Cook time: 8 minutes

Ingredients:

- 235 ml shredded Mozzarella cheese
- ¼ medium red pepper, seeded and chopped
- 120 ml chopped fresh spinach leaves
- 2 tablespoons chopped black olives
- 2 tablespoons crumbled feta cheese

Instructions:

1. Sprinkle Mozzarella into an ungreased round non-stick baking dish in an even layer.
2. Add remaining ingredients on top.
3. Place dish into air fryer basket. Adjust the temperature to 176ºC and bake for 8 minutes, checking halfway through to avoid burning.
4. Top of pizza will be golden brown, and the cheese melted when done.
5. Remove dish from fryer and let cool 5 minutes before slicing and serving.

Crispy Cabbage Steaks

Serves 4

Prep time: 5 minutes / Cook time: 10 minutes

Ingredients:

- 1 small head green cabbage, cored and cut into ½-inch-thick slices
- ¼ teaspoon salt
- ¼ teaspoon ground black pepper
- 2 tablespoons olive oil
- 1 clove garlic, peeled and finely minced
- ½ teaspoon dried thyme
- ½ teaspoon dried parsley

Instructions:

1. Sprinkle each side of cabbage with salt and pepper, then place into ungreased air fryer basket, working in batches if needed.
2. Drizzle each side of cabbage with olive oil, then sprinkle with remaining ingredients on both sides.
3. Adjust the temperature to 176ºC and air fry for 10 minutes, turning "steaks" halfway through cooking.
4. Cabbage will be browned at the edges and tender when done.
5. Serve warm.

White Cheddar and Mushroom Soufflés

Serves 4

Prep time: 15 minutes / Cook time: 12 minutes

Ingredients:

- 3 large eggs, whites and yolks separated
- 120 ml extra mature white Cheddar cheese
- 85 g soft white cheese
- ¼ teaspoon cream of tartar
- ¼ teaspoon salt
- ¼ teaspoon ground black pepper
- 120 ml chestnut mushrooms, sliced

Instructions:

1. In a large bowl, whip egg whites until stiff peaks form, about 2 minutes.
2. In a separate large bowl, beat Cheddar, egg yolks, soft white cheese, cream of tartar, salt, and pepper together until combined.
3. Fold egg whites into cheese mixture, being careful not to stir.

4. Fold in mushrooms, then pour mixture evenly into four ungreased ramekins.
5. Place ramekins into air fryer basket.
6. Adjust the temperature to 176ºC and bake for 12 minutes.
7. Eggs will be browned on the top and firm in the centre when done.
8. Serve warm.

Roasted Vegetable Mélange with Herbs

Serves 4

Prep time: 10 minutes / Cook time: 14 to 18 minutes

Ingredients:

- 1 (230 g) package sliced mushrooms
- 1 yellow butternut squash, sliced
- 1 red pepper, sliced
- 3 cloves garlic, sliced
- 1 tablespoon olive oil
- ½ teaspoon dried basil
- ½ teaspoon dried thyme
- ½ teaspoon dried tarragon

Instructions:

1. Preheat the air fryer to 176ºC.
2. Toss the mushrooms, squash, and pepper with the garlic and olive oil in a large bowl until well coated.
3. Mix in the basil, thyme, and tarragon and toss again.
4. Spread the vegetables evenly in the air fryer basket and roast for 14 to 18 minutes, or until the vegetables are fork-tender.
5. Cool for 5 minutes before serving.

Air Fryer Veggies with Halloumi

Serves 2

Prep time: 5 minutes / Cook time: 14 minutes

Ingredients:

- 2 courgettes, cut into even chunks
- 1 large aubergine, peeled, cut into chunks
- 1 large carrot, cut into chunks
- 170 g halloumi cheese, cubed
- 2 teaspoons olive oil
- Salt and black pepper, to taste
- 1 teaspoon dried mixed herbs

Instructions:

1. Preheat the air fryer to 172ºC.
2. Combine the courgettes, aubergine, carrot, cheese, olive oil, salt, and pepper in a large bowl and toss to coat well.
3. Spread the mixture evenly in the air fryer basket and air fry for 14 minutes until crispy and golden, shaking the basket once during cooking.
4. Serve topped with mixed herbs.

Parmesan Artichokes

Serves 4

Prep time: 10 minutes / Cook time: 10 minutes

Ingredients:

- 2 medium artichokes, trimmed and quartered, centre removed
- 2 tablespoons coconut oil
- 1 large egg, beaten
- 120 ml grated vegetarian Parmesan cheese
- 60 ml blanched finely ground almond flour
- ½ teaspoon crushed red pepper flakes

Instructions:

1. In a large bowl, toss artichokes in coconut oil and then dip each piece into the egg.
2. Mix the Parmesan and almond flour in a large bowl.
3. Add artichoke pieces and toss to cover as completely as possible, sprinkle with pepper flakes.
4. Place into the air fryer basket.
5. Adjust the temperature to 204°C and air fry for 10 minutes.
6. Toss the basket two times during cooking.
7. Serve warm.

Baked Courgette

Serves 4

Prep time: 10 minutes / Cook time: 8 minutes

Ingredients:

- 2 tablespoons salted butter
- 60 ml diced white onion
- ½ teaspoon minced garlic
- 120 ml double cream
- 60 g full fat soft white cheese
- 235 ml shredded extra mature Cheddar cheese
- 2 medium courgette, spiralized

Instructions:

1. In a large saucepan over medium heat, melt butter.
2. Add onion and sauté until it begins to soften, 1 to 3 minutes.
3. Add garlic and sauté for 30 seconds, then pour in cream and add soft white cheese.
4. Remove the pan from heat and stir in Cheddar.
5. Add the courgette and toss in the sauce, then put into a round baking dish.
6. Cover the dish with foil and place into the air fryer basket.
7. Adjust the temperature to 188°C and set the timer for 8 minutes.
8. After 6 minutes remove the foil and let the top brown for remaining cooking time. Stir and serve.

Bacon-Wrapped Shrimp and Jalapeño

Serves 8

Prep time: 20 minutes / Cook time: 26 minutes

Ingredients:

- 24 large shrimp, peeled and deveined, about 340 g
- 5 tablespoons barbecue sauce, divided
- 12 strips bacon, cut in half
- 24 small pickled jalapeño slices

Instructions:

1. Toss together the shrimp and 3 tablespoons of the barbecue sauce. Let stand for 15 minutes. Soak 24 wooden toothpicks in water for 10 minutes. Wrap 1 piece bacon around the shrimp and jalapeño slice, then secure with a toothpick.
2. Preheat the air fryer to 176°C.
3. Working in batches, place half of the shrimp in the air fryer basket, spacing them ½ inch apart. Air fry for 10 minutes. Turn shrimp over with tongs and air fry for 3 minutes more, or until bacon is golden brown and shrimp are cooked through.
4. Brush with the remaining barbecue sauce and serve.

Vegetable Pot Stickers

Makes 12 pot stickers

Prep time: 12 minutes / Cook time: 11 to 18 minutes

Ingredients:

- 240 ml shredded red cabbage
- 60 ml chopped button mushrooms
- 60 ml grated carrot

- 2 tablespoons minced onion
- 2 garlic cloves, minced
- 2 teaspoons grated fresh ginger
- 12 gyoza/pot sticker wrappers
- 2½ teaspoons olive oil, divided

Instructions:

1. In a baking pan, combine the red cabbage, mushrooms, carrot, onion, garlic, and ginger. Add 1 tablespoon of water. Place in the air fryer and air fry at 188°C for 3 to 6 minutes, until the vegetables are crisp-tender. Drain and set aside.
2. Working one at a time, place the pot sticker wrappers on a work surface. Top each wrapper with a scant 1 tablespoon of the filling. Fold half of the wrapper over the other half to form a half circle. Dab one edge with water and press both edges together.
3. To another pan, add 1¼ teaspoons of olive oil. Put half of the pot stickers, seam-side up, in the pan. Air fry for 5 minutes, or until the bottoms are light golden brown. Add 1 tablespoon of water and return the pan to the air fryer.
4. Air fry for 4 to 6 minutes more, or until hot. Repeat with the remaining pot stickers, remaining 1¼ teaspoons of oil, and another tablespoon of water. Serve immediately.

Hush Puppies

Serves 12

Prep time: 45 minutes / Cook time: 10 minutes

Ingredients:

- 240 ml self-raising yellow cornmeal
- 120 ml plain flour
- 1 teaspoon sugar

- 1 teaspoon salt
- 1 teaspoon freshly ground black pepper
- 1 large egg
- 80 ml canned creamed corn
- 240 ml minced onion
- 2 teaspoons minced jalapeño pepper
- 2 tablespoons olive oil, divided

Instructions:

1. Thoroughly combine the cornmeal, flour, sugar, salt, and pepper in a large bowl.
2. Whisk together the egg and corn in a small bowl. Pour the egg mixture into the bowl of cornmeal mixture and stir to combine. Stir in the minced onion and jalapeño. Cover the bowl with plastic wrap and place in the refrigerator for 30 minutes.
3. Preheat the air fryer to 192°C. Line the air fryer basket with parchment paper and lightly brush it with 1 tablespoon of olive oil.
4. Scoop out the cornmeal mixture and form into 24 balls, about 1 inch.
5. Arrange the balls in the parchment paper-lined basket, leaving space between each ball.
6. Air fry in batches for 5 minutes. Shake the basket and brush the balls with the remaining 1 tablespoon of olive oil. Continue cooking for 5 minutes until golden brown.
7. Remove the balls (hush puppies) from the basket and serve on a plate.

Crispy Cajun Dill Pickle Chips

Makes 16 slices

Prep time: 5 minutes / Cook time: 10 minutes

Ingredients:

- 60 ml plain flour
- 120 ml panko breadcrumbs
- 1 large egg, beaten
- 2 teaspoons Cajun seasoning
- 2 large dill pickles, sliced into 8 rounds each
- Cooking spray

Instructions:

1. Preheat the air fryer to 200°C.
2. Place the plain flour, panko breadcrumbs, and egg into 3 separate shallow bowls, then stir the Cajun seasoning into the flour.
3. Dredge each pickle chip in the flour mixture, then the egg, and finally the breadcrumbs. Shake off any excess, then place each coated pickle chip on a plate.
4. Spritz the air fryer basket with cooking spray, then place 8 pickle chips in the basket and air fry for 5 minutes, or until crispy and golden brown. Repeat this process with the remaining pickle chips.
5. Remove the chips and allow to slightly cool on a wire rack before serving.

Soft white cheese Stuffed Jalapeño Poppers

Serves 10

Prep time: 12 minutes / Cook time: 6 to 8 minutes

Ingredients:

- 227 g soft white cheese, at room temperature
- 240 ml panko breadcrumbs, divided
- 2 tablespoons fresh parsley, minced
- 1 teaspoon chilli powder
- 10 jalapeño peppers, halved and seeded
- Cooking oil spray

Instructions:

1. In a small bowl, whisk the soft white cheese, 120 ml of panko, the parsley, and chilli powder until combined. Stuff the cheese mixture into the jalapeño halves.
2. Sprinkle the tops of the stuffed jalapeños with the remaining 120 ml of panko and press it lightly into the filling.

3. Insert the crisper plate into the basket and the basket into the unit. Preheat the unit by selecting AIR FRY, setting the temperature to 192ºC, and setting the time to 3 minutes. Select START/STOP to begin.
4. Once the unit is preheated, spray the crisper plate with cooking oil. Place the poppers into the basket.
5. Select AIR FRY, set the temperature to 192ºC, and set the time to 8 minutes. Select START/STOP to begin.
6. After 6 minutes, check the poppers. If they are softened and the cheese is melted, they are done. If not, resume cooking.
7. When the cooking is complete, serve warm.

Honey-Mustard Chicken Wings

Serves 2

Prep time: 10 minutes / Cook time: 24 minutes

Ingredients:

- 907 g chicken wings
- Salt and freshly ground black pepper, to taste
- 2 tablespoons butter
- 60 ml honey
- 60 ml spicy brown mustard
- Pinch ground cayenne pepper
- 2 teaspoons Worcestershire sauce

Instructions:

1. Prepare the chicken wings by cutting off the wing tips and discarding (or freezing for chicken stock). Divide the drumettes from the wingettes by cutting through the joint. Place the chicken wing pieces in a large bowl.
2. Preheat the air fryer to 204ºC.
3. Season the wings with salt and freshly ground black pepper and air fry the wings in two batches for 10 minutes per batch, shaking the basket halfway through the

cooking process.
4. While the wings are air frying, combine the remaining ingredients in a small saucepan over low heat.
5. When both batches are done, toss all the wings with the honey-mustard sauce and toss them all back into the basket for another 4 minutes to heat through and finish cooking. Give the basket a good shake part way through the cooking process to redistribute the wings. Remove the wings from the air fryer and serve.

Lebanese Muhammara

Serves 6

Prep time: 15 minutes / Cook time: 15 minutes

Ingredients:

- 2 large red peppers
- 60 ml plus 2 tablespoons extra-virgin olive oil
- 240 ml walnut halves
- 1 tablespoon agave nectar or honey
- 1 teaspoon fresh lemon juice
- 1 teaspoon ground cumin
- 1 teaspoon rock salt
- 1 teaspoon red pepper flakes
- Raw vegetables (such as cucumber, carrots, courgette slices, or cauliflower) or toasted pitta chips, for serving

Instructions:

1. Drizzle the peppers with 2 tablespoons of the olive oil and place in the air fryer basket. Set the air fryer to 204ºC for 10 minutes.
2. Add the walnuts to the basket, arranging them around the peppers. Set the air fryer to 204ºC for 5 minutes.
3. Remove the peppers, seal in a resealable plastic bag, and let rest for 5 to 10 minutes. Transfer the walnuts to a plate and set aside

to cool.

4. Place the softened peppers, walnuts, agave, lemon juice, cumin, salt, and ½ teaspoon of the pepper flakes in a food processor and purée until smooth.

5. Transfer the dip to a serving bowl and make an indentation in the middle. Pour the remaining 60 ml olive oil into the indentation. Garnish the dip with the remaining ½ teaspoon pepper flakes.

6. Serve with vegetables or toasted pitta chips.

Garlic Edamame

Serves 4

Prep time: 5 minutes / Cook time: 10 minutes

Ingredients:

- Olive oil
- 1 (454 g) bag frozen edamame in pods
- ½ teaspoon salt
- ½ teaspoon garlic salt
- ¼ teaspoon freshly ground black pepper
- ½ teaspoon red pepper flakes (optional)

Instructions:

1. Spray the air fryer basket lightly with olive oil.

2. In a medium bowl, add the frozen edamame and lightly spray with olive oil. Toss to coat.

3. In a small bowl, mix together the salt, garlic salt, black pepper, and red pepper flakes (if using). Add the mixture to the edamame and toss until evenly coated.

4. Place half the edamame in the air fryer basket. Do not overfill the basket.

5. Air fry at 192ºC for 5 minutes. Shake the basket and cook until the edamame is starting to brown and get crispy, 3 to 5 more minutes.

6. Repeat with the remaining edamame and serve immediately.

Onion Pakoras

Serves 2

Prep time: 30 minutes / Cook time: 10 minutes per batch

Ingredients:

- 2 medium brown or white onions, sliced (475 ml)
- 120 ml chopped fresh coriander
- 2 tablespoons vegetable oil
- 1 tablespoon chickpea flour
- 1 tablespoon rice flour, or 2 tablespoons chickpea flour
- 1 teaspoon ground turmeric
- 1 teaspoon cumin seeds
- 1 teaspoon rock salt
- ½ teaspoon cayenne pepper
- Vegetable oil spray

Instructions:

1. In a large bowl, combine the onions, coriander, oil, chickpea flour, rice flour, turmeric, cumin seeds, salt, and cayenne. Stir to combine. Cover and let stand for 30 minutes or up to overnight. (This allows the onions to release moisture, creating a batter.) Mix well before using.

2. Spray the air fryer basket generously with vegetable oil spray. Drop half of the batter in 6 heaping tablespoons into the basket. Set the air fryer to 176ºC for 8 minutes. Carefully turn the pakoras over and spray with oil spray. Set the air fryer for 2 minutes, or until the batter is cooked through and crisp.

3. Repeat with remaining batter to make 6 more pakoras, checking at 6 minutes for doneness. Serve hot.

Roasted Mushrooms with Garlic

Serves 4

Prep time: 3 minutes / Cook time: 22 to 27 minutes

Ingredients:

- 16 garlic cloves, peeled
- 2 teaspoons olive oil, divided
- 16 button mushrooms
- ½ teaspoon dried marjoram
- ⅛ teaspoon freshly ground black pepper
- 1 tablespoon white wine or low-salt vegetable broth

Instructions:

1. In a baking pan, mix the garlic with 1 teaspoon of olive oil. Roast in the air fryer at 176°C for 12 minutes.
2. Add the mushrooms, marjoram, and pepper. Stir to coat. Drizzle with the remaining 1 teaspoon of olive oil and the white wine.
3. Return to the air fryer and roast for 10 to 15 minutes more, or until the mushrooms and garlic cloves are tender. Serve.

Lemon-Pepper Chicken Drumsticks

Serves 2

Prep time: 30 minutes / Cook time: 30 minutes

Ingredients:

- 2 teaspoons freshly ground coarse black pepper
- 1 teaspoon baking powder
- ½ teaspoon garlic powder
- 4 chicken drumsticks (113 g each)
- Rock salt, to taste
- 1 lemon

Instructions:

1. In a small bowl, stir together the pepper, baking powder, and garlic powder. Place the drumsticks on a plate and sprinkle evenly with the baking powder mixture, turning the drumsticks so they're well coated. Let the drumsticks stand in the refrigerator for at least 1 hour or up to overnight.
2. Sprinkle the drumsticks with salt, then transfer them to the air fryer, standing them bone-end up and leaning against the wall of the air fryer basket. Air fry at 192°C until cooked through and crisp on the outside, about 30 minutes.
3. Transfer the drumsticks to a serving platter and finely grate the zest of the lemon over them while they're hot. Cut the lemon into wedges and serve with the warm drumsticks.

Easy Roasted Chickpeas

Prep time: 5 minutes / Cook time: 15 minutes / Makes about 240 ml

Ingredients:

- 1 (425 g) can chickpeas, drained
- 2 teaspoons curry powder
- ¼ teaspoon salt
- 1 tablespoon olive oil

Instructions:

1. Drain chickpeas thoroughly and spread in a single layer on paper towels. Cover with another paper towel and press gently to remove extra moisture. Don't press too hard or you'll crush the chickpeas.
2. Mix curry powder and salt together.
3. Place chickpeas in a medium bowl and sprinkle with seasonings. Stir well to coat.
4. Add olive oil and stir again to distribute oil.
5. Air fry at 200°C for 15 minutes, stopping to shake basket about halfway through cooking time.
6. Cool completely and store in airtight container.

Lemony Endive in Curried Yoghurt

Serves 6

Prep time: 5 minutes / Cook time: 10 minutes

Ingredients:

- 6 heads endive
- 120 ml plain and fat-free yoghurt
- 3 tablespoons lemon juice
- 1 teaspoon garlic powder
- ½ teaspoon curry powder
- Salt and ground black pepper, to taste

Instructions:

1. Wash the endives and slice them in half lengthwise.
2. In a bowl, mix together the yoghurt, lemon juice, garlic powder, curry powder, salt and pepper.
3. Brush the endive halves with the marinade, coating them completely. Allow to sit for at least 30 minutes or up to 24 hours.
4. Preheat the air fryer to 160°C.
5. Put the endives in the air fryer basket and air fry for 10 minutes.
6. Serve hot.

Goat Cheese and Garlic Crostini

Serves 4

Prep time: 3 minutes / Cook time: 5 minutes

Ingredients:

- 1 wholemeal baguette
- 60 ml olive oil
- 2 garlic cloves, minced
- 113 g goat cheese
- 2 tablespoons fresh basil, minced

Instructions:

1. Preheat the air fryer to 192°C.
2. Cut the baguette into ½-inch-thick slices.
3. In a small bowl, mix together the olive oil and garlic, then brush it over one side of each slice of bread.
4. Place the olive-oil-coated bread in a single layer in the air fryer basket and bake for 5 minutes.
5. Meanwhile, in a small bowl, mix together the goat cheese and basil.
6. Remove the toast from the air fryer, then spread a thin layer of the goat cheese mixture over the top of each piece and serve.

Spicy Tortilla Chips

Serves 4

Prep time: 5 minutes / Cook time: 8 to 12 minutes

Ingredients:

- ½ teaspoon ground cumin
- ½ teaspoon paprika
- ½ teaspoon chilli powder
- ½ teaspoon salt
- Pinch cayenne pepper
- 8 (6-inch) corn tortillas, each cut into 6 wedges
- Cooking spray

Instructions:

1. Preheat the air fryer to 192°C. Lightly spritz the air fryer basket with cooking spray.
2. Stir together the cumin, paprika, chilli powder, salt, and pepper in a small bowl.
3. Working in batches, arrange the tortilla wedges in the air fryer basket in a single layer. Lightly mist them with cooking spray. Sprinkle some seasoning mixture on top of the tortilla wedges.
4. Air fry for 4 to 6 minutes, shaking the basket halfway through, or until the chips are lightly browned and crunchy.
5. Repeat with the remaining tortilla wedges and seasoning mixture.
6. Let the tortilla chips cool for 5 minutes and serve.

CHAPTER 9 DESSERTS

Butter and Chocolate Chip Cookies

Serves 8

Prep time: 20 minutes / Cook time: 11 minutes

Ingredients:

- 110 g unsalted butter, at room temperature
- 155 g powdered sweetener
- 60 g chunky peanut butter
- 1 teaspoon vanilla paste
- 1 fine almond flour
- 75 g coconut flour
- 35 g cocoa powder, unsweetened
- 1 ½ teaspoons baking powder
- ¼ teaspoon ground cinnamon
- ¼ teaspoon ginger
- 85 g unsweetened, or dark chocolate chips

Instructions:

1. In a mixing dish, beat the butter and sweetener until creamy and uniform. Stir in the peanut butter and vanilla.
2. In another mixing dish, thoroughly combine the flour, cocoa powder, baking powder, cinnamon, and ginger.
3. Add the flour mixture to the peanut butter mixture; mix to combine well. Afterwards, fold in the chocolate chips. Drop by large spoonsful onto a baking paper-lined air fryer basket. Bake at 185°C for 11 minutes or until golden brown on the top. Bon appétit!

Apple Fries

Serves 8

Prep time: 10 minutes / Cook time: 7 minutes

Ingredients:

- Coconut, or avocado oil, for spraying
- 110 g plain flour
- 3 large eggs, beaten
- 100 g crushed digestive biscuits
- 55 g granulated sugar
- 1 teaspoon ground cinnamon
- 3 large Gala apples, peeled, cored and cut into wedges
- 240 ml caramel sauce, warmed

Instructions:

1. Preheat the air fryer to 192°C. Line the air fryer basket with baking paper and spray lightly with oil.
2. Place the flour and beaten eggs in separate bowls and set aside. In another bowl, mix together the crushed biscuits, sugar and cinnamon.
3. Working one at a time, coat the apple wedges in the flour, dip in the egg and then dredge in the biscuit mix until evenly coated.
4. Place the apples in the prepared basket, taking care not to overlap, and spray lightly with oil. You may need to work in batches, depending on the size of your air fryer.
5. Cook for 5 minutes, flip, spray with oil, and cook for another 2 minutes, or until crunchy and golden brown.
6. Drizzle the caramel sauce over the top and serve.

Simple Apple Turnovers

Serves 4

Prep time: 10 minutes / Cook time: 10 minutes

Ingredients:

- 1 apple, peeled, quartered, and thinly sliced
- ½ teaspoons pumpkin pie spice
- Juice of ½ lemon
- 1 tablespoon granulated sugar
- Pinch of kosher, or coarse sea salt
- 6 sheets filo pastry

Instructions:

1. Preheat the air fryer to 164°C.
2. In a medium bowl, combine the apple, pumpkin pie spice, lemon juice, granulated sugar, and kosher salt.
3. Cut the filo pastry sheets into 4 equal pieces and place individual tablespoons of apple filling in the center of each piece, then fold in both sides and roll from front to back.
4. Spray the air fryer basket with nonstick cooking spray, then place the turnovers in the basket and bake for 10 minutes or until golden brown.
5. Remove the turnovers from the air fryer and allow to cool on a wire rack for 10 minutes before serving.

Almond-Roasted Pears

Serves 4

Prep time: 10 minutes / Cook time: 15 to 20 minutes

Ingredients:

- Yogurt Topping:
- 140-170 g pot vanilla Greek yogurt
- ¼ teaspoon almond flavoring
- 2 whole pears
- 4 crushed Biscoff biscuits
- 1 tablespoon flaked almonds

- 1 tablespoon unsalted butter

Instructions:

1. Stir the almond flavoring into yogurt and set aside while preparing pears.
2. Halve each pear and spoon out the core.
3. Place pear halves in air fryer basket, skin side down.
4. Stir together the crushed biscuits and almonds. Place a quarter of this mixture into the hollow of each pear half.
5. Cut butter into 4 pieces and place one piece on top of biscuit mixture in each pear.
6. Roast at 184°C for 15 to 20 minutes, or until pears have cooked through but are still slightly firm.
7. Serve pears warm with a dollop of yogurt topping.

Cream-Filled Sponge Cakes

Makes 4 cakes

Prep time: 10 minutes / Cook time: 10 minutes

Ingredients:

- Coconut, or avocado oil, for spraying
- 1 tube croissant dough
- 4 cream-filled sponge cake fingers
- 1 tablespoon icing sugar

Instructions:

1. Line the air fryer basket with baking paper, and spray lightly with oil.
2. Unroll the dough into a single flat layer and cut it into 4 equal pieces.
3. Place 1 sponge cake in the center of each piece of dough. Wrap the dough around the cake, pinching the ends to seal.
4. Place the wrapped cakes in the prepared basket, and spray lightly with oil.
5. Bake at 92°C for 5 minutes, flip, spray with oil, and cook for another 5 minutes, or until

golden brown.

6. Dust with the icing sugar and serve.

Coconut-Custard Pie

Serves 4

Prep time: 10 minutes / Cook time: 20 to 23 minutes

Ingredients:

- 240 ml milk
- 50 g granulated sugar, plus 2 tablespoons
- 30 g scone mix
- 1 teaspoon vanilla extract
- 2 eggs
- 2 tablespoons melted butter
- Cooking spray
- 50 g desiccated, sweetened coconut

Instructions:

1. Place all ingredients except coconut in a medium bowl.
2. Using a hand mixer, beat on high speed for 3 minutes.
3. Let sit for 5 minutes.
4. Preheat the air fryer to 164ºC.
5. Spray a baking pan with cooking spray and place pan in air fryer basket.
6. Pour filling into pan and sprinkle coconut over top.
7. Cook pie for 20 to 23 minutes or until center sets.

Baked Cheesecake

Serves 6

Prep time: 30 minutes / Cook time: 35 minutes

Ingredients:

- 50 g almond flour
- 1½ tablespoons unsalted butter, melted
- 2 tablespoons granulated sweetener
- 225 g cream cheese, softened
- 25 g powdered sweetener

- ½ teaspoon vanilla paste
- 1 egg, at room temperature
- Topping:
- 355 ml sour cream
- 3 tablespoons powdered sweetener
- 1 teaspoon vanilla extract

Instructions:

1. Thoroughly combine the almond flour, butter, and 2 tablespoons of granulated sweetener in a mixing bowl. Press the mixture into the bottom of lightly greased custard cups.
2. Then, mix the cream cheese, 25 g of powdered sweetener, vanilla, and egg using an electric mixer on low speed. Pour the batter into the pan, covering the crust.
3. Bake in the preheated air fryer at 164ºC for 35 minutes until edges are puffed and the surface is firm.
4. Mix the sour cream, 3 tablespoons of powdered sweetener, and vanilla for the topping; spread over the crust and allow it to cool to room temperature.
5. Transfer to your refrigerator for 6 to 8 hours. Serve well chilled.

Pineapple Galette

Serves 2

Prep time: 15 minutes / Cook time: 40 minutes

Ingredients:

- ¼ medium-size pineapple, peeled, cored, and cut crosswise into ¼-inch-thick slices
- 2 tablespoons dark rum, or apple juice
- 1 teaspoon vanilla extract
- ½ teaspoon kosher, or coarse sea salt
- Finely grated zest of ½ lime
- 1 store-bought sheet puff pastry, cut into an 8-inch round
- 3 tablespoons granulated sugar
- 2 tablespoons unsalted butter, cubed and

chilled

- Coconut ice cream, for serving

Instructions:

1. In a small bowl, combine the pineapple slices, rum, vanilla, salt, and lime zest and let stand for at least 10 minutes to allow the pineapple to soak in the rum.
2. Meanwhile, press the puff pastry round into the bottom and up the sides of a cake pan and use the tines of a fork to dock the bottom and sides.
3. Arrange the pineapple slices on the bottom of the pastry in a more or less single layer, then sprinkle with the sugar and dot with the butter. Drizzle with the leftover juices from the bowl. Place the pan in the air fryer and bake at 154°C until the pastry is puffed and golden brown and the pineapple is lightly caramelized on top, about 40 minutes.
4. Transfer the pan to a wire rack to cool for 15 minutes. Unmold the galette from the pan and serve warm with coconut ice cream.

Brownies for Two

Serves 2

Prep time: 5 minutes / Cook time: 15 minutes

Ingredients:

- 50 g blanched finely ground almond flour
- 3 tablespoons granulated sweetener
- 3 tablespoons unsweetened cocoa powder
- ½ teaspoon baking powder
- 1 teaspoon vanilla extract
- 2 large eggs, whisked
- 2 tablespoons salted butter, melted

Instructions:

1. In a medium bowl, combine flour, sweetener, cocoa powder, and baking powder.
2. Add in vanilla, eggs, and butter, and stir until

a thick batter forms.

3. Pour batter into two ramekins greased with cooking spray and place ramekins into air fryer basket. Adjust the temperature to 164°C and bake for 15 minutes. Centers will be firm when done. Let ramekins cool 5 minutes before serving.

Coconut Mixed Berry Crisp

Serves 6

Prep time: 5 minutes / Cook time: 20 minutes

Ingredients:

- 1 tablespoon butter, melted
- 340 g mixed berries
- 65 g granulated sweetener
- 1 teaspoon pure vanilla extract
- ½ teaspoon ground cinnamon
- ¼ teaspoon ground cloves
- ¼ teaspoon grated nutmeg
- 50 g coconut chips, for garnish

Instructions:

1. Preheat the air fryer to 164°C. Coat a baking pan with melted butter.
2. Put the remaining ingredients except the coconut chips in the prepared baking pan.
3. Bake in the preheated air fryer for 20 minutes.
4. Serve garnished with the coconut chips.

Chocolate Bread Pudding

Serves 4

Prep time: 10 minutes / Cook time: 10 to 12 minutes

Ingredients:

- Nonstick, flour-infused baking spray
- 1 egg
- 1 egg yolk
- 175 ml chocolate milk

- 2 tablespoons cocoa powder
- 3 tablespoons light brown sugar
- 3 tablespoons peanut butter
- 1 teaspoon vanilla extract
- 5 slices firm white bread, cubed

Spray a 6-by-2-inch round baking pan with the baking spray. Set aside.

2. In a medium bowl, whisk the egg, egg yolk, chocolate milk, cocoa powder, brown sugar, peanut butter, and vanilla until thoroughly combined. Stir in the bread cubes and let soak for 10 minutes. Spoon this mixture into the prepared pan.

3. Insert the crisper plate into the basket and the basket into the unit. Preheat the unit to 164°C.

4. cook the pudding for about 10 minutes and then check if done. It is done when it is firm to the touch. If not, resume cooking.

5. When the cooking is complete, let the pudding cool for 5 minutes. Serve warm.

Air Fryer Cinnamon Sugar Dessert Fries

Serves: 4

Prep Time: 10 minutes / Cook Time: 10 minutes

Ingredients:

- 2 medium sweet potatoes, peeled and cut into fries
- 1 tbsp (15ml) vegetable oil
- ¼ cup (50g) granulated sugar
- 1 tsp (2g) ground cinnamon
- ¼ tsp (1g) salt
- ¼ cup (60g) unsalted butter, melted

Instructions:

1. Preheat your air fryer to 200°C.
2. In a large mixing bowl, toss the sweet potato fries with the vegetable oil until evenly coated.

3. In a separate bowl, mix together the sugar, cinnamon, and salt.

4. Place the sweet potato fries in the air fryer basket in a single layer and air fry for 10 minutes or until crispy and golden brown.

5. Once the sweet potato fries are done, remove them from the air fryer and immediately toss them in the melted butter.

6. Sprinkle the cinnamon sugar mixture over the fries and toss again until evenly coated. Serve immediately and enjoy!

Protein Powder Doughnut Holes

Makes 12 holes

Prep time: 25 minutes / Cook time: 6 minutes

Ingredients:

- 50 g blanched finely ground almond flour
- 60 g low-carb vanilla protein powder
- 100 g granulated sweetener
- ½ teaspoon baking powder
- 1 large egg
- 5 tablespoons unsalted butter, melted
- ½ teaspoon vanilla extract

Instructions:

1. Mix all ingredients in a large bowl. Place into the freezer for 20 minutes.

2. Wet your hands with water and roll the dough into twelve balls.

3. Cut a piece of baking paper to fit your air fryer basket. Working in batches as necessary, place doughnut holes into the air fryer basket on top of baking paper.

4. Adjust the temperature to 192°C and air fry for 6 minutes.

5. Flip doughnut holes halfway through the cooking time.

6. Let cool completely before serving.

Apple Wedges with Apricots

Serves 4

Prep time: 5 minutes / Cook time: 15 to 18 minutes

Ingredients:

- 4 large apples, peeled and sliced into 8 wedges
- 2 tablespoons light olive oil
- 95 g dried apricots, chopped
- 1 to 2 tablespoons granulated sugar
- ½ teaspoon ground cinnamon

Instructions:

1. Preheat the air fryer to 180°C.
2. Toss the apple wedges with the olive oil in a mixing bowl until well coated.
3. Place the apple wedges in the air fryer basket and air fry for 12 to 15 minutes.
4. Sprinkle with the dried apricots and air fry for another 3 minutes.
5. Meanwhile, thoroughly combine the sugar and cinnamon in a small bowl.
6. Remove the apple wedges from the basket to a plate. Serve sprinkled with the sugar mixture.

Baked Apples and Walnuts

Serves 4

Prep time: 6 minutes / Cook time: 20 minutes

Ingredients:

- 4 small Granny Smith apples
- 50 g chopped walnuts
- 50 g light brown sugar
- 2 tablespoons butter, melted
- 1 teaspoon ground cinnamon
- ½ teaspoon ground nutmeg
- 120 ml water, or apple juice

Instructions:

1. Cut off the top third of the apples. Spoon out the core and some of the flesh and discard. Place the apples in a small air fryer baking pan.
2. Insert the crisper plate into the basket and the basket into the unit. Preheat to 176°C.
3. In a small bowl, stir together the walnuts, brown sugar, melted butter, cinnamon, and nutmeg. Spoon this mixture into the centers of the hollowed-out apples.
4. Once the unit is preheated, pour the water into the crisper plate. Place the baking pan into the basket.
5. Bake for 20 minutes.
6. When the cooking is complete, the apples should be bubbly and fork tender.

Printed in Great Britain
by Amazon

21194806R00052